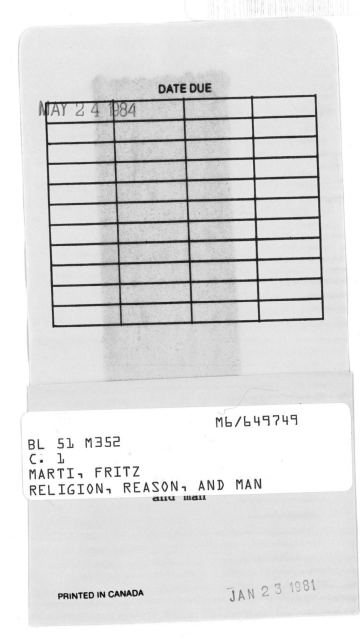

DATE DUE

MAY 2 4 1984			

RELIGION, REASON AND MAN

Fritz Marti

RELIGION,
REASON
AND
MAN

By

FRITZ MARTI

Professor Emeritus
Southern Illinois University
Edwardsville, Illinois

WARREN H. GREEN, INC.
St. Louis, Missouri, U.S.A.

Published by

WARREN H. GREEN, INC.
10 South Brentwood Blvd.
St. Louis, Missouri 63105

© 1974, by Fritz Marti

Library of Congress Catalog No. 74-9353
I.S.B.N. No. 0-87527-141-3

Printed in the United States of America

To my students
without whom this book could not have been written
and
to my ever-helpful critic, Gertrude Austin Marti

PREFACE

Students would like to *know*. There are voluminous books which leave them with the impression that no knowledge can be obtained from philosophy, that philosophical thinking on religion must be non-committal, and that there is no solid basis for a serious commitment. Yet, students seek a firm stand, be it inside some ecclesiastic fold or out.

This little book tries to present in plain language some of the basic insights occidental philosophy has found during these 2500 years. Philosophy looks for *truth*. Its purpose is *not to find fault*. To be sure, the untutored often bring forth formulations which cover up a truth instead of expressing it clearly. Then, teaching must point the way to better expressions. And this service must be tendered to both believers and unbelievers, so that the sincere faith of both may be confirmed.

Many of our young people are sorely perplexed. In the summer of 1970, the Department of Philosophical Studies at Southern Illinois University in Edwardsville introduced a course called "Religion, Reason and Man," designed as a tutorial in the elements of philosophy of religion. The course has been very popular. In my sections, I soon felt the need for pithy readings and especially for a very concise handbook. The present text was used in the fall of 1972 and it broke a log-jam of questions. My students wrote hundreds of them. I have made use of a good number, as topics for commentaries on each chapter.

One way of using this book is to read all the chapters first, and then, for a second reading, to go from the marginal numbers to the corresponding questions. However, it is also possible to read all the questions first, by way of staking out the ground to be cultivated, and then to read the chapters as a kind of harvest from that ground. A third way starts from the Index.

vii

Obviously, this short treatise offers only an introduction. But without some such introductory explanation, a reader who believes that philosophical reflection produces nothing but hypothetical theories is likely to miss the point of the great books whose authors wrote from a conviction that reason demands a personal stand. They did not write for the sake of mere academic debate. *Truth* calls for *commitment,* and commitment to the truth makes one free.

I owe a word of thanks to my friend and colleague Charles Anthony Corr who, in 1970, as chairman of our department, collaborated in launching our new course, gave it its name, and has now consented to my use of that name as the title of this book.

As I already said, my method of evaluating books on religion is not infallible. I have come across a work of crucial importance for our topic, and I advise the reader to consult at least its Chapter 4: *The Sin of Idolatry.* The author is Theodore Roszak and the title *Where the Wasteland Ends* (Anchor Book A 903, Doubleday & Co., 1973).

SIGNS AND QUOTATIONS

The numbers in parentheses, in the left margin of the text, refer to the respective student questions, and vice versa.

Quotations identified only by volume and page number in parentheses indicate where the passage can be found in:

Fichte's sämmtliche Werke (Mayer Müller, Leipzig, n.d.)	Vols. I-VIII
NW = nachgelassene Werke	Vols. I-III
Hegel's Werke (Duncker und Humbolt, Berlin 1832-40)	Vols. I-XVIII
Schelling's sämmtliche Werke (J. G. Cotta, Stuttgart 1856-61)	I-X
NW = nachgelassene Werke	Vols. I-IV

Kant's *Critique of Pure Reason* is quoted from the 1787 edition, so-called B. Other quotations are specifically identified.

Where not otherwise indicated, translations are the author's own.

CONTENTS

RELIGION, REASON AND MAN

INTRODUCTION

"Are you aware of the danger which you are incurring? If you were going to commit your body to some one who might do good or harm to it, would you not carefully consider and ask the opinion of your friends and kindred, and deliberate many days as to whether you should give him the care of your body? But when the soul is in question, which you hold to be of far more value than the body, and upon the good or evil of which depends the well-being of your all, about this you never consulted either with your father or with your brother or with any one of us who are your companions. But no sooner does this foreigner appear, than you instantly commit your soul to his keeping."

Plato: *Protagoras* 313ab (Jowett's translation). (Socrates' warning to young Hippocrates who wants to become the pupil of Protagoras, just arrived.)

"What sort of philosophy one chooses depends on what sort of man one is; for a philosophical system is not a dead piece of furniture that we can reject or accept as we wish; it is rather a thing animated by the soul of the person who holds it. A person indolent by nature or dulled and distorted by mental servitude, learned redundancy, and vanity will never raise himself to the level of idealism. We can show the dogmatist the inadequacy and incoherence of his system, . . . but we cannot convince him because he is incapable of calmly receiving and coolly assessing a teaching which he absolutely cannot endure."

Fichte: *First Introduction to the Science of Knowledge* (Werke I, 434f) 1797. (Translated by John Lachs, Appleton-Century-Crofts, 1970, 16.)

"Give man the awareness of what he is and soon he will also learn to be what he should be. Give him theoretical self-respect and the practical self-respect will soon

(2)

follow. One would hope in vain for any great progress of mankind as a result of the mere good will of man, because in order to become better he would have had to be good already. For that very reason the revolution in man has to emanate from the consciousness of his being, he must be good theoretically in order to become so practically."

Schelling: *About the I as the Principle of Philosophy.* (I,157) 1795.

◆ ◆ ◆

In 1959, E. Z. Friedenberg wrote about *The Vanishing Adolescent* and defined adolescence as the time when a young person ought to find himself or herself. In our 1970's, finding oneself has become the war cry of many young people. Some seem to believe that, without taking cognizance of the findings of great minds through the ages, they can reach their goal either by lonely meditation or else by endless talk with equally uninformed contemporaries. A few fanatics harbor the illusion that their generation is the first one to be aware of the relevance of growing up, and thus they view anything in print as irrelevant to their own search. Yet all the while they are making use of the language they have learned from their elders and of the ideas conveyed by the words of that language. They may dislike the ideas and simply reject them, not realizing that the rejection

(3) leaves the ideas unchanged and undigested. The typical example is he who proclaims that "God is dead." He does not pause to ask himself what he means by his word "God." It is not his own word; he has simply adopted the meaning put forward by his opponent whose fundamentalism he hates. So his proclamation amounts to a retention of his dead God.

Finding oneself means maturing. And maturing does not come about by juvenile negativism. It comes by bold inquiry. Ideas hateful to us must have had acceptable meanings for their adherents. What were those meanings in their time? And what kind of people can find the ideas significant, and so find themselves in terms of those ideas? Of course, such questions are dangerous. You risk finding that ideas you once considered hateful are now significant in your own life. You may be "converted." This is what has happened to many a Jesus Freak these last years. If you do not like the prospect of conversion, should you not ask yourself *why* you feel your dislike is justified? If it is a matter of mere feeling, is not the Freak quite justified in following his feeling for the Jesus who has entered his life as guide and redeemer? Suppose it happened to you. After all, your feelings might change, and then you would find conversion a boon. For so it is for those in need of that kind of guidance. What is it that guides *you*? What do you really believe? Who *are* you anyway? Is *your* mind a piece of flotsam buffeted by waves of feeling which break over you? Or is there *really* any true knowledge you can have of yourself?

The question of truth is worth asking. And unless you ask it, there is no answer. The answer does not hover in the air like clouds or smog or atomic fallout, nor does it exist in space like gravity or magnetism. It exists in the mind where, indeed, its formulations do change in line with the demands of intellectual conscience, and with the mental needs of individuals. This existence of ever new answers to serious problems is what may be called the life of truth. Religionists have called it the presence of the Spirit, and they have rightly attributed authority to the Spirit. The authority of truth is manifest in the fact that we cannot dodge nor escape the question as to what is true.

We cannot evade it even in the case of the lowliest truths, like those of arithmetic. How much is 123 plus 456? You say you are not interested and, for the moment, this may be quite true since you may have more serious things on your mind. Yet, does not the arithmetical problem rankle? Can you swat and kill it like a mosquito? Have you not already looked for and found the answer—579? And how did you find it? You added 3 and 6, 2 and 5, 1 and 4. Or, being sharper than such school routine, you may have realized at a glance that each of these additions amounts to less than ten, and you may have started by adding the hundreds and then the tens, and then the ones. At all events, you have not made the question vanish. You have gotten it out of your mind by solving it.

It is the authority of real questions, no matter how simple or how complex, that have demanded solutions. It may take hundreds of years, but the question is there. It may have to be reformulated in order to be solvable. And the reformulation of the question of religion is the task that confronts us here. It is the question which will not loose its hold upon us unless it is solved. And the solution, too, has a hold upon us. This is manifest in the fact that solutions, once formulated, demand reformulations which bring the old truths into line with the newly available knowledge. Thus, our knowledge regarding the rotation of the earth explains, yet does not annihilate, the old knowledge that the sun rises and sets.

Man's dim feeling that his mind stands under an authority which he has called a "God" is verified and substantiated, not annihilated, by the philosophical reflection which is the core of all worthwhile theology. When man came to speak of a personal God with whom he felt a personal relationship, he had a new formula for the fact that he, personally, was addressed by authority. And when the great theologian, St. Augustine, found his equation "God is the Truth"* (it is not a reversible equation, since Augustine's God is also goodness and beauty**) he lifted the anthropomorphic formula "God is Person" into the purer realm of verifiable reflection. He *verified,* he *did not annihilate* whatever was true in the old formula.

Verification is the task of philosophy. Intended (though

---

*Augustinus: *de libero arbitrio* XII,xv,39. Tu autem concesseras, si quid supra mentes nostras esse monstrarem, Deum te esse confessurum, si adhuc nihil esset superius. ... Si enim aliquid est excellentius, ille potius Deus est: si autem non est, iam ipsa veritas Deus est.

(If I show to you that there is something superior to our minds, you will concede that it is God, provided there should be nothing higher. ... If, however there is something more excellent, that rather is God. If there is nothing more excellent then the truth itself is already God.)

Confessions VI,x,16. O aeterna veritas et vera caritas et cara aeternitas! Tu es deus meus, tibi suspiro *die ac nocte* (Psalm 1:2).

(Oh, eternal truth and true love and beloved eternity! Thou art my God, to thee I aspire day and night.

**de natura boni*, vii. Rationalibus spiritibus hoc praestitit Deus ut si nolint, corrumpi non possint; id est si obedientiam conservaverint sub Domino Deo suo, ac si incorruptibili pulchritudini eius adhaeserint.

(God granted to rational spirits that they could not be corrupted if they did not want to be, that is, if they would maintain proper obedience under their Lord God and would adhere to his incorruptible beauty.)

de Trinitate, VIII,ii,4. Donum hoc et bonum illud. Tolle hoc et illud, et vide ipsum bonum si potes. ... Sic amandus est deus, non hoc et illud bonum sed ipsum bonum.

(This good and that good. Take away the 'this' and 'that' and regard good itself if you can. ... Thus God is to be loved, not this and that good, but good itself.)

always unsuccessful) annihilation is what juvenile minds hope to accomplish. Bless their hearts! For they are serious. They do seek the truth. But they are not serious enough. They are allergic to work. They will not bother to study. They have not yet decided to enter the humble ranks of scholars. They want to swallow THE Truth, in one gulp. They still lack the scholarly humility of going from one little truth to the next. Their juvenile exorbitance has always been at the core of religious

(4) enthusiasm. The result is well known; each religion claims to have the whole truth—by painless revelation, not by painful study.

Owing partly to two world wars and their aftermath, our age has become uncomfortably aware of the fact that the internecine war of the religions (including, of course, the Marxist religion) is obsolete and must be replaced by scholarly discussion. And the technique of such discussion must be learned, just like that of any up-to-date discussion in any one of the natural sciences. It is not a do-it-yourself job. True, only if you yourself put your mind to the task can anything fruitful result. But the task remains without issue if you do not inform yourself as to what kind of discussion is up-to-date.

The chief part of such information is found in historical study. Perhaps even the few pages you have just read may make you aware of what St. Augustine meant when he said "the soul is the life of the body, and God is the life of the soul."*** Remember his formula *Deus veritas* (God = truth).

(5) Also remember that the search for the truth is a personal enterprise. Therefore, the preliminary question: Where do *you* stand, as of now, and who is fit to be *your* guide? There is no ideal teacher. I may be good for you and bad for another student. And even if I can help you now, you will (let us hope!) outgrow me and my formulations. Nor is there any final book. There are only good books and bad. Good are those which help you for the time being. (It may be a very long time; the truly great teachers have presided over centuries of inquiry, nor do they ever entirely retire from the field.) Bad are the books

---

***de libero arbitrio,* II,vi,41. Sicut enim tota vita corporis est anima, sic beata vita animae deus est.

(As the soul is whole life of the body, so is God the blessed life of the soul.)

which cleverly though maybe unintentionally keep you from being up-to-date. Do not waste your time reading bad books. So much for a start!

Student Questions

(1) Q: I understand why a private college or university that is connected with a certain religious belief would offer a course about "Religion, Reason and Man." Why, and what advantage does a *state* university have to offer this course?

A: Because we want to give students the help they feel they need. The course has attracted students from the very beginning when, in the summer of 1970, it was first offered experimentally. Why does the university offer the service of several physicians and a pharmacy? Because students are not always in the best of health. In the same way, many are sorely perplexed with regard to religion, as the steady enrollment in this course shows. The beliefs in which they have been brought up do not seem to have provided them with the intellectual vitamins they have come to need. So, as far as the individual student is concerned, you can regard this course as a kind of dispensary. Just as a health service would like to bring the individual up to par physically, we would like to bring him or her up to date intellectually so that beliefs or unbelief do not remain fixed in a form which turns out to be obsolete and therefore blocks the very endeavor of religion to make life vigorous and joyful.

As for the state, it is not a person and therefore has no conscience. Only individuals can be conscientious. That is one of the reasons why the higher religions have insisted on being independent of the state, so that human conscience can be free. Nevertheless, justice demands that there be good laws and an efficient administration. And, in one way, legislatures, administrations and courts are organized to function as what could be called the conscience of the state. However, these organizations are also functions of the state itself, and since the state as such cannot be conscientious, its organs more or less easily approve of the state as is, uncritically. Thus, there is need of a careful and fair critique of the state from outside. Of course, it is the prime duty of every citizen to furnish such critique. But the majority are not usually well equipped for that difficult task. It requires not only maturity but scholarship. There have been times when the church officially acted as the critic of the state, as the state's conscience. At times, it still does so in our century. Yet, often it lacks the scholarly detachment and knowledge. Therefore, one might argue that the university ought to function as the state's conscience. Of course, the university is no person either. It is a group either of fairly accomplished or of incipient scholars. And scholarship is conscientiousness. In our case, we propose to have a conscientious look at religion, taking our stand on available knowledge.

(2) Q: What is meant by "good" in the quotation from Schelling: Man "must be theoretically good in order to become so practically"?

A.   Good is what he ought to be.—Your question shows your theoretical awareness that you ought to understand what you read. That awareness induces you to ask the question, and your act of asking it makes you a good student in practice.

"Give man the awareness of what he is and he will also learn to be what he ought to be." By his own actions, he ought to be a responsible person instead of being flotsam adrift on the billows of his mere feelings. In short, he ought to take himself in hand. This he cannot do as long as he conceives of himself as a fortuitous combination of cells, or a bubbling kettle of emotions. He must first ask himself the main question of our Chapter II: Who am I as I? What do I truly mean when I say as little as the simple word "I" insofar as it refers to myself? (see below, page 14).

Anticipating the answer to that question, I will add this preview. One of the main troubles of our time is the fact that, being fascinated with the useful results of natural science, we have taught that man is nothing but a complex organism and, consequently, that self-criticism is verbiage, and self-control an illusion. This teaching has made many a youngster (and oldster too) "incapable of calmly receiving and cooly assessing a teaching which he absolutely cannot endure," as Fichte says. He cannot endure the insight that "I am I for myself alone," and "nobody can be I for me." Even less can he endure the corrollary that it is precisely this being really oneself which makes possible the community with others. He has been indoctrinated to the point where he would rather believe he is "a piece of lava in the moon," as Fichte also said (Werke I,175*). The result is the disintegration of society. Our honestly worried conservatives sincerely preach a return to mythological formulae. But they do not warn against the objectivism which allows such formulae (like "soul," "eternal punishment," "heavenly reward") to be taken literally and made unbelievable. That, in turn, is what has led to the seemingly more believable objectivism of the more fashionable scientistic doctrines.

Scientific study of man is necessary and indispensable in our time. But it can neither replace the mythological imagery of religion, nor lead to a true understanding of religiosity. That understanding requires philosophical reflection which, in turn, must start from the meaning of I.

(3)   Q: I can understand why a group would say, "there is no God," but how can a group logically say, "God is dead"?

    A: All the gods of the past who ever "lived," that is, held sway over their faithful, have "died," that is, they have lost their hold on even the last believer. However, when gods "die" they do not simply vanish. They still exist as historical entities in men's memories and in works of art and literary documents. Memory may turn them into demons; this happened to the Greek and Roman gods during the Christian middle ages. In the Renaissance, these gods revived; their images were appreciated though not worshipped, by men of culture. Similarly, a modern un-

believer can very well appreciate the image of Jehovah, of
the Holy Trinity, and also of foreign gods like Brahma and
Allah. Still, for the unbeliever they are "dead," and his
appreciation is not worship. The Renaissance appreciators
of the old gods were almost all good Christian believers.
And the modern unbeliever is not necessarily safe against a
resurrection of Jehovah or the Trinity in his own mind. For
the gods do retain the capacity of reviving. (See C. G.
Jung's 1936 paper on the resuscitation of Wodan among
the Nazi.)

Ninety years ago (1881-83), Nietzsche brought forth
his Zarathustra who, in the Preface, meets an old hermit in
the forest praising his God with songs, tears, laughter and
muttering. Having left him, Zarathustra said in his heart:
"Is it possible? This old saint in his forest has not yet
heard that God is dead!" Nietzsche believed that the end of
Christianity had come. So did Marx before him. But the
Christian religion is still more than a literary memory.

After all, every believer of every religion is "reborn"
in it, and thus it revives in him. Today, the burning
question is, what is the innermost life of religion, the "life
of God," or, to speak with Augustin, the life of truth? And
both believer and unbeliever had better ponder this question, making use of every pertinent religious image and
philosophical insight.

(4) Q: You have used the word religion. How do you define
        it?

     A: For a start, let us simply go back to the Latin root of
        the word. It comes (so some of the ancients said) from the
        verb *ligere*, to tie. And *re-ligio* is the tying back, that is,
        what ties us back into our origin. The latter is God, if you
        do not mind this mythological word. Schelling says (Werke
        XI,186), "People ask: how does human consciousness come
        to God? But consciousness does not come to God; its very
        first movement is away from the true God." This is why
        the religions preach conversion. The word comes from
        vertere, to turn, and *conversio* is a clear turnabout, from

running away to coming back. The hasidic rabbis speak of *Umkehr,* turning around. However, this problem will occupy us later.

(5) Q: You mentioned that, like our search for truth, religion is a very personal and private thing. If this is true, which I also believe, isn't all organized religion useless as well as harmful?

A: Any organization, meant to be useful, turns out to be useful in certain respects. Like everything human, it can also be harmful. The harm often results when an organization takes itself to be its own justification instead of taking itself as a tool. Religion, meant to proclaim and serve divinity, at times declares itself divine, and that is what breeds harm.

It is an old story. In his didactic poem *On the Nature of Things,* Lucretius, who died 55 or 54 B.C., spoke of life "oppressed under severe religion" (I,63) and, having described some religious atrocities, "criminal and impious deeds performed by religion itself" (I,83), exclaims, "to so many evils could religion persuade!" (I,101) *Tantum religio potuit suadere malorum!*

Everybody can easily see such harmful effects. It is not so easy, at least nowadays, for people not at home in philosophy, to point out in what way religion can be beneficial, which is one of our tasks in this study.

Chapter I

DOUBT AND SELFCERTAINTY

My brother, do you really want to go into seclusion?
Do you want to seek the way to yourself? Pause a while
and listen.

"He who seeks has easily lost himself. All seclusion
is guilt." Thus says the herd. And for a long time you
belonged to the herd.

The voice of the herd will still find an echo in you.
And even if you retort saying, "I no longer have your
conscience," it will be a lamentation and a pain.

Behold, this pain itself is born from that common
conscience whose last glow is reflected in your misery.

But you want to walk the way of your misery which
is the way to yourself! Therefore, show me your qualifica-
tion for it, and your strength!

Are you a new power and a new law? An original
movement? A self-turning wheel? Can you force stars to
revolve about you?

Alas, there is so much hankering for height! There
are so many spasms of ambition! Show me that you are
not one of those who hanker and itch!

Alas, there are so many haughty thoughts. They do
what bellows do, they inflate you and make you emptier.

You call yourself free? Let me hear your ruling
thought, and do not tell me you have escaped from under a
yoke.

(6)

Are you one who is entitled to escape from a yoke?
Many a one threw away his remaining worthiness when he
threw away his servitude.

Free? Free from what? What does Zarathustra care!
But look me in the eye and let your candid regard tell me,
free for what?

Nietzsche: Thus Spoke Zarathustra. First Part (section 17):
"About the Way of the Creative One." The entire section is
worth reading.

#

11

"I believe; help my unbelief!" Mark 9:24.

"Everyone who understands that he is doubting knows something that is true, and he is certain of this fact. Therefore he is certain of what is true. Everyone, therefore, who doubts that there is truth has in himself something true of which he does not doubt." Augustinus: *de vera religione,* xxxix,73. *(See the Latin original, our page 105*.)*

"Who can doubt that he lives, understands, wants, reflects, knows, judges? Indeed, even if he doubts, he lives; if he doubts, he knows that he is doubting; if he doubts he wants to be certain; if he doubts he reflects; if he doubts he knows that he does not know; if he doubts he judges that he must not rashly consent." Augustinus: *de Trinitate,* X,x,14.

◆——◆——◆

Everybody agrees that religion is a personal matter. Of course, there is the ulterior question as to its social significance and society's responsibility for religion. That question will concern us later.

Religion concerns you as a responsible person. Animals do not seem to have religion. Some have rituals. Some baboons gather in a herd at sunrise, excitedly greeting the sun. Call it sun worship if you will. It remains the kind of ritual which one simply does without asking for a reason. But man is a rational animal. He asks: *"Why* am I doing this? What end will it accomplish?" The shouting of the baboons has no ulterior end. It is what they *must* do at sunrise, and that is all. Must you go to church? Must you pray? Must you ask what your life is all about?

When you ask, "What am I here for?", it is a rational question. It is your own personal question. It is not a ritual which you perform as a member of the herd. It is you who want to know. It is you who wonder. And when you doubt that there is a purpose to your life, it is you who doubt. Nobody can doubt for you. Your very doubt is an affirmation of your personal identity. Of the latter you are certain. You cannot be equally certain of me, especially when what I say seems unreasonable, or what I do inconsistent. But when you doubt the integrity of your own actions or the soundness of your own mind, you are still certain of your own identity.

Even if you are afflicted with schizophrenia and seem to be split into two personalities, it is still one and the same you who is now of one mind and then of another. It is the same Dr. Jekyll who oddly turns into Mr. Hyde. Everybody can be a bit of a schizophrenic. "For I do not understand what I do, for it is not what I wish that I do, but what I hate, that I do. . . . For I do not do the good that I wish, but the evil that I do not wish" (Romans 7:15 and 19). Nor can you blame it on somebody else. The second half of the verse last quoted says it is "the sin that dwells in me." Mythologically speaking, you can call it a devil which possesses you and, which, within you, makes war against you. Yet you must confess with St. Paul that "I see another law in *my* members, warring against the law of *my* mind and making me prisoner to the law of sin that is in my members" (Romans 7:23). You cannot get away from it; these recalcitrant members are part of you and, if you wish to use the word sin, it is *your* sin, not anybody else's.

The easy device of the revivalist who starts with what he assumes to be your inherent sinfulness is no tool for the philosopher. Philosophical reflection goes deeper. It makes us aware of the personal identity, in the saint as well as the sinner. So let us reflect and ask: What do we mean by "person"? But let us be careful lest we get wrapped up in academic jargon. Let us talk plain English. For the word "person" is really too impersonal. It means anybody, not you specifically. Let us ask a plainer question. Just exactly what do you mean when, referring to yourself, you say "I"?

(7)   What can you say of this *I* of yours, simply as *I*?

Now, you have gone to school, and you have been taught to be objective. So you feel tempted to objectify this "I" of yours. You may be inclined to argue as follows. "The word *I* designates my personality which is the product of heredity and environment. It designates a specific and (I am even proud to say) very complex unit of mankind, as it were; a molecule of humanity, the objective study of which must be entrusted to the trained psychologist. Society designates this unit by the name, John Doe. As for myself, for convenience sake, I designate it by the simple pronoun *I*." Beautiful speech! Unfortunately it is beside the point. It dodges the question. It talks about you not as an *I* but as some *It*. Please, do not misunderstand. It is far from my intention to deny the existence of the complex unit which may puzzle even you yourself to the point where you need the help of your head shrinker. Facts are facts, and each one of us finds himself inhabiting his *me*. And the complexity of that *me* is quite a problem, indeed. Around 500 B.C. Heraclitus said: "You would not find out the boundaries of soul, even by traveling along every path, so deep a measure does it have." (Kirk and Raven: *The Presocratic Philosophers*, p. 183; Diels fragment 45). Our contemporary investigations of the subconscious confirm this. Our question, however, is not psychological nor psychoanalytic. It is philosophical. Let us ask again:

(8)　　　What do you mean when you say *I*? And what words can adequately express this meaning? What can you truthfully say?

All human speech is historically conditioned. Our words have their changing history and so have our ideas. None of us has created the language he speaks. We borrow our terminology from our predecessors although we do coin new words and change the meaning of old ones. Knowing this, I need not apologize for making use of formulations which have been put forward by the philosophers. In the case of our question, I shall turn to Fichte who, trying to be quite plain, used the kind of plain language I shall quote.

But for you, any language will remain unintelligible, as long as you assume that the talk is about Fichte's *I*, or about mine. The question is addressed to *you*. What can you say of *your I*? Say this, and ask whether it is true:

"*Nobody else can be I for me. I am I for myself alone.* I alone can experience *my* feelings, make *my* decisions, think *my* thoughts."

The quotation marks are appropriate provided you are doing what you are here supposed to do. You must read these sentences as being yours, not mine. In fact, of course, they *are* yours if you but read them with an alert mind, not with a mind

dulled by schooling and thus made docile and almost impersonal. Philosophy teaches no impersonal doctrines. It puts before
you sentences you are supposed to read as if they were your
own. You must ask yourself, "Can I truthfully say this about
myself?" Can anybody else be *I* for you? Can I be *I* for anyone
else? If you merely memorize the quoted sentences and file
them away as Fichte's doctrine, you deprive them of their
meaning. They mean you or else they are meaningless.

If I say *you*, of course I mean any reader who is awake and
alert, and willing to test the truth of the statements. Are they
(9)   true of yourself? If so, then we may reasonably assume that
they are true of every other reader who asks himself what he
means when he says *I*.

It is possible, of course, that you may not find the
statements in quotation marks to your taste. In that case, you
are not only at liberty, you are under logical obligation to think
up more precise, more truthful statements, provided you have at
least understood the question and caught the drift of the quoted
answers.

Sad to say, it is also possible that your schooling has made
you deaf to the question or, worse, that your moral depravity
has brought you to the point where you can no longer say *I*
honestly, where you have been imprisoned in the straightjacket
of your *me* and, therefore, have completely identified yourself
with that bottomless "soul" of which Heraclitus spoke. In that
case, you are indeed ready for the psychoanalyst, and it will be
his Herculean task to reawaken in yourself the courage to say *I*.
(Nowadays, the psychoanalyst seems to have taken over the task
of the spiritual adviser whose function is misinterpreted as if he
were a salesman of insurance against perdition or a secret agent
of the celestial police.)

Instead of dwelling on such sad possibilities, let us get back
to our own task which is to weigh the formulations quoted and
to ask whether they are true. And this is the point where the
efficacy of writing stops unless the writer may rightfully assume
that the reader is still with him. This means the writer must
assume that the reader has learned to be his own teacher and
therefore will be able or at least desirous of taking the side of
the writer and, having thus discovered what the writer really

means, be ready to defend that meaning against mistaken imputations. In our case, such an imputation would be the assumption that we are dealing only with some particular *I*, like
(10)   Fichte's or mine or the *I* of the specific reader.

     In contrast to writing, oral teaching can pretty quickly correct the student's misunderstandings, provided the student cooperates and voices his misgivings. However a student's indolence or inarticulateness prevents even oral teaching.
(11)   So, back to our question and to some of its implication. "I am I for myself alone." Some existentialists have drawn the mistaken conclusion that I am locked up in myself. Jean Paul Sartre has written a very gripping play, *Huis Clos* (No Exit), in which the three characters are each caught in his or her individuality and, in their coexistence, they are each other's hell. But the conclusion is wrong, and the opposite statement marks the truth; just because I am I, and to just the extent to which I know it, just that far am I *open* to other selves. If my talk were merely jabber, how could you understand me? To be sure, you could imitate it if you were a jabberer yourself, and you might enjoy the imitation. Yet it would be an enjoyment of sound, not of understanding. Understanding springs from the critical
(12)   question: What do you *mean*? Every meaning is a form of selfcertainty.

     This brings up the second main formulation of Fichte: I cannot be aware of myself as an *I* without, at the same time, distinguishing my *I* from whatever is *Not-I*. When I discover that, in fact, I am I for myself alone, then while I realize that my words do state the truth and that the truth is manifest in them, I also distinguish the words from the reality of *I*, for I know full well that other words could express the same truth. (For instance, Descartes' *cogito sum,* meaning: I, as I, am in a state of awareness and it is that awareness which is, in fact, my being as an *I*; "being aware, I *am*.") I realize that my words are not I.
(13)   I cannot be aware of myself, as an *I*, without distinguishing myself from some *not-I*. At the very least, I must admit that I am not identical with the words which express my self-awareness. Words are sound but I am not a sound. Words can be written on paper; what I mean by "I" is nothing written; I am

the one who, reading the words, grasps their meaning. This is a distinction, it is not a separation between the meaning and the expression thereof. I cannot be aware of myself as an I without some kind of expression, be it even as little as an almost inarticulate feeling, or be it a mythological word like soul or

(15) spirit, or a psychological word like mind or consciousness, or a philosophical formulation like "I am I for myself alone." Such expressions are the first and minimal kind of *not-I* which inevitably comes with my awareness of "I."

You see that this little bit of philosophical reflection was required for seeing this first kind of *not-I*. It is much easier to see the second kind, by means of an ordinary reflection which almost everybody makes sooner or later. Reflect and ask: What is required for my having words at all, speaking them silently or aloud, and writing them down? The answer is obvious, I must be incarnate; I must have this body of mine with a nervous system, a mouth, and fingers. Also I must have an environment which furnishes me with the words of a language.

And that environment amounts to the third kind of *not-I*, the physical and historical reality. In the physical world, I discover other living bodies; and like myself, they have their history which goes back through the generations. Most people find plants and animals more interesting than rocks and stars; likewise humans with whom we can talk are more real than corpses. A corpse can be laid alongside another, but two corpses cannot occupy the same space; they are mutually exclusive. Living beings, however, can communicate. Lifeless things can only bump into each other. Understanding is possible only between selves, even animal selves.

This, of course, does not yet shed any light on the mystery of our incarnation nor on the wider mystery of all biological life. But it does give occasion to look briefly at what I have just

(16) called the first and second kinds of *not-I*, and what I will simply
(17) call the *me*, the unique body and mind of mine. Biology and
(18) psychology can and must study *me* which, for them, is an objective reality. The subjective aspect of my *me* is confined to my experience. On his part a biologist or a psychologist can make use of his empathy and feel his way into another living

(19) being, just as the artist and the actor and anyone who feels

(20) sympathy does. We need such empathy to understand each other's words the way they are meant. (Words, of course, are historically conditioned, and historical knowledge is needed to understand them, at least the knowledge we all have of the words our society uses.)

(21) Every meaning is a form of selfcertainty. Therefore even radical doubt expresses the certainty of truth. How can anyone say "I doubt this" and mean it, unless he contrasts "this" with whatever may happen to be the truth, which he does not know but which he certainly assumes as existing? And how can he say and mean it without being certain that it is he who doubts? To doubt means to assert one's own integrity as a thinker and a responsible person. For it is our responsibility not to believe what does not seem to be true, and it is our responsibility to ask appropriate questions (at least in our mind, if not in public) in order to ascertain the truth, if possible. To be sure, in many a subject matter, we may find that we are not prepared to formulate a pertinent question. In that case, it is our responsibility to suspend judgment till the time when we may be properly prepared.

The Greek verb *sképtomai* literally means to lean upon, figuratively to rely upon; *sképtesthai* means to put up a prop, therefore figuratively, to pretend. The noun *sképsis* can mean a pretence, but in philosophy it came to mean the cautious withholding of judgment. Therefore all careful thinking is skeptical. In the *Critique of Pure Reason* (451) Kant says that, in a disputation, the skeptical method will "investigate whether the topic itself may not be a mere illusion." He also points out (*Ibid.* 789) that, in matters of pure reason, "the first step is dogmatic and marks the tender age" of the mind, whereas "the second step is skeptical and shows a cautious judgment made wise by experience. However a third step is necessary, one which pertains to a mature, manly judgment." For "skepticism is only a place of rest for human reason, where it can reflect on its dogmatic peregrination" and ascertain where it now stands, in order to find a safer path forward; "but it is not a place of residence, for such a place can be found only in a full certainty, be it of the topics themselves or of the limits of our knowledge thereof." In other words, skepticism is a halfway house between dogmatism and philosophy which is tenable because it is critical. Here, we are seeking the latter.

(22)
(23)

Student Questions

(6) Q: "Are you one who is entitled to escape from a yoke? Many a one threw away his remaining worthiness when he threw away his servitude." (Nietzsche) Does servitude mean organized religion? Does it mean believing in something greater than one's self?

A: Yes, both can be examples of servitude. In his Zarathustra (Part III, "Of old and new tablets," 4.) Nietzsche writes: "He who cannot command his own self shall obey. And many a one can issue commands to himself yet be far from obeying them." And (Part I, "About war and warriors"): "Rebellion is noble in a slave. Let your nobility be obedience! Let your commanding be an obeying!" Again, in *The Dawn of Day* (60.): "One takes pride in obeying, and this is what distinguishes all aristocrats." Furthermore, in *Beyond Good and Evil* (188.): "Let it be said again that what seems to be essential 'in heaven and on earth' is that there be obedience for a long time and in one and the same direction." (Read the entire section 188.)

Highminded servitude lifts man above his petty selfishness. Nietzsche agrees with the ennobling challenge to serve "something greater than one's self," as you put it.

But of course there is also a kind of servitude which does not ennoble, the servitude of the slave who obeys in order to flatter his master from whom he expects favors, here and hereafter. And only too often does organized religion cater to such selfish minds. Yet, one should not generalize as Nietzsche does when he says flatly "the values of the church are those of slaves" (Oktavausgabe XIII,309).

His Zarathustra, however, says to his disciples that, "although the priests are my enemies, my blood is akin to theirs, and I want my blood honored even in theirs. I suffer and have suffered with them," for they bear "the fetters of false values and of illusion." (loc. cit. Second Part, section 4.)

(7) Q: Why does each individual have an I?

A: Each one of us can answer: "because only I can *be* I." What is the alternative that seems to be on your mind? Something like an octopus but with millions of arms instead of eight? Now, if you watch an octopus it looks indeed as if each arm had its own life and was moving independently from the "head office." You will have to ask a zoologist whether there is good evidence that the animal knows what its arms are doing. If it does, you can ask again whether each arm also knows. Asking mythologically, does each arm have a soul of its own, and what is the relation of that arm soul to the head soul of the whole animal? Or you may turn to a botanical image, where the independence of the parts of a plant at times seems obvious; snip off a twig, put it in a glass of water, and it will sprout roots so that soon you can give this new plant its own pot.

But let us get back to your question. Maybe you have it upside down. Only by starting with "I am I for myself alone" can you arrive at individuality in the fullest sense. (I am not saying you must start with an explicitly clear awareness of what "I" means. You need not have philosophical explicitness. What is required is the identity of a self, such as you express it when somebody tries to pin something to a garment of yours and pushes the pin into your skin, whereupon you exclaim, "Hey, that's me!")

In short, instead of telling you, "because only I can *be* I," I might say: "I do not *have* an I, I *am* I." There are not two of me, the one who *has* his I and the other who *is* it. For, as our chapter tries to show, the *I* is no *It*.

(8) Q: Why is it that every individual's "I" is different from everybody else's, and yet all share things in common? Example: All seek happiness, for his or her "I."

A: Your example would seem to annihilate the sharing. Your happiness is yours and mine is mine, and they are not had "in common"; they are two happinesses. True, we can be happy together, even happy simply because we are together, but each must experience his own happiness. As long as I am unconscious you cannot share your happiness with me.

As for your real question regarding "things in common," we can share them just because we are different selves; I am I, and you are you. How else could your question mean anything to you? How else could I understand it?

(9) Q: "Nobody else can be I for me. I am I for myself alone." If so, with what justification can I say that, these statements being true with regard to myself, "we may reasonably assume that they are true for every other 'self'"? I do not feel very comfortable about that assumption.

A: Why do you feel uneasy? There must be a reason for that feeling. Perhaps you are ignoring the second half of the sentence in the text which speaks only of the reader "who asks himself what he means when he says I." If he so asks, how can he possibly believe he could "be I for anyone else" than himself?—True, if you are thinking of those who do not ask the critical question and who therefore can well imagine they are things, not selves—odd things like "a piece of lava on the moon" (2)—you have a good reason for feeling uncomfortable. You cannot "reasonably assume" that they distinguish between *I* and *It*. Fichte says a man who conceives of himself as an *It* instead of an *I* lacks "the very requirement of all philosophizing. Anyone who is not yet at one with himself on this point has no understanding of any fundamental philosophy, and needs none. Nature, whose machine he is, will lead him, even without his own cooperation, into all the occupations that are his to pursue. Philosophizing calls for independence, and this one can only confer on oneself." (*Founda-*

tions of the Entire Science of Knowledge; I,175*; translation by Peter Heath, Appleton-Century-Crofts 1970, p.
162.)

(10) Q: How can I prove to others that I am I? How can I
prove my "being" if only I can experience my "self"?

A: You are asking for the impossible. Formally, there can
be no proof "for others." What we mean by "proof" is the
certainty found by the self for the self. Materially you do
prove that you are a nice guy, by your deeds, or that you
are thinking, by your clearly formulated questions or
statements.
Each one of us must become clear in his own mind.
And only thus can we ever understand each other. As for
our *I*, since only I can experience myself, you likewise
must experience your self for yourself. The kind of
"proof" you have in mind would turn the self into a thing,
the *I* into a *not-I*.
Schelling's *Aphorism* 31 (of 1805; Werke VII,146)
says: "One cannot describe reason to anybody; reason must
describe itself in each one and through each one."

(11) Q: Is all this purely a question of semantics?

A: Yes indeed, insofar as the wording is concerned. But
so are all statements man ever makes. However, the relativi-
ty of the wording (e.g., the fact that this is English, not
German, nor Latin) does not annihilate the logical meaning
which the words manifest more or less clearly.

(12) Q: Would you explain again the meaning of the statement, "Every meaning is a form of selfcertainty."

A: Every meaning is (at least potentially) meaningful for
someone who means it. To be sure, some meanings, e.g., a
scientific truth not yet discovered, are what they are
without being (as yet) actually meant by anybody. But *if*
meant, then the one who means it experiences certainty
and it is he himself who does so. He becomes more certain
of himself as a scientist.

(13) Q: In the first chapter (pages 15-17) I get the strange impression that I am not me. Please clear me up on this.

      A: Making philosophical distinctions often gives one a strange impression. Your question reminds me of an unexpected incident during my graduate years. My mother was not given to philosophizing, but once, while we were waiting for a streetcar, she suddenly said, "You know, I sometimes wonder why I am me."
              As an *I*, I am for myself alone, a strictly private entity, as it were. As an *I*, I experience my *me* as mine. And as mine, the *me* is also of private dignity; we usually resent it if others treat our body as if they were at liberty to do so, pushing, pinching, etc. We even resent, at times, their intrusion on the privacy of our mind, trying to teach us a lesson, or asking for information we would rather withhold. We say: None of your business! Nevertheless, my *me*, my body, my strength, my mental ability, even my knowledge, is public property in a sense; it can all be investigated, by physicians, psychologists, policemen, examining teachers. To be sure, others may misjudge my "me," but so do I quite often. What, at first glance, may

(14)   seem strange to you is that each one of us ought to be critical of his *me*, so that there seems to be an outright separation between the *me* in the docket, and the interpreting or indicting *I*. In fact we do so judge our *me*. How else could we ever improve in any respect? The *me*, of course, often resists the improvement the *I* would bring about. I am then faced by *me* as if by a stranger. And if despondent I may wish I had a quite different *me*. We even daydream about living in another place and time. See (17) below.
              If you were to make the philosophical mistake of taking the distinction between the *I* and the *me* as a separation then your strange impression would be fully justified. In short, although I *am* not me, yet my *me* is definitely mine, not yours nor anybody else's.

(14) Q: You once said (13) that "I" is the director and "me" the directed. Also that the word hell may mean a mental state. If Paul's statement, "I do not do the good that I

wish, but the evil that I do not wish" (Romans 7:19) is true, how then can I be responsible for the hell I may create?

A: Who else is responsible? Some devil? "The law of sin that is in my members" (Romans 7:23) may be considered a disease, but it is a moral one of my making.

(15) Q: Can I assume that the "I" to which we have referred is what religions would call the "soul" of an individual, and the "me" what they would call the physical part of the individual or his body?

A: Quite so, for a first round of reflection. However, such mythological terms can also mislead you into blaming your mistakes on your body or on your mind. Many religions will then warn you that the soul ought to direct both body and mind. It is the soul that leads itself into perdition.

(16) Q: Does being the "me" sometimes help one to find the "I"? For instance, many indulge in drugs because of inferiority complexes or insecurities. They want to belong to something, to identify with something or somebody. Some never find themselves. On the other hand, some may find that the role they are thus playing isn't really what they want to do, and then they may arrive at their real and true "I."

A: Very true. Putting it a little more pedantically, they find that their drug addiction was an endeavor to renege on the responsibility of the *I*, and now they embrace that responsibility.

(17) Q: Is it necessary to make the distinction between I and me? If so why? It appears that among the majority of us each looks at himself, as a whole in one being, only distinguishing between body and soul which, for many, is only an assumption.

A: What do you mean by "necessary"?—(a) Logically possible? Yes, as I tried to show. (b) Required of everybody? By whom? If by his conscience or his curiosity, yes. But, as you point out, some are not interested and shrug off the question as "only an assumption." (c) Personally necessary? I am inclined to say yes, without qualification, for I do believe that anybody who flatly identifies his *I* with his *me* has either lost the zest for living or else is in danger of being caught in his *me* as in a straightjacket, with neurotic results. I do admit that there are specimens of men and women so splendidly one with the *me* that they look like healthy animals in their wilderness or, if you prefer, like sleepwalking saints guided by their guardian angel. However, an animal in the wilderness must constantly adjust its *me* to the circumstances. As for the saint, he had better keep praying God to keep the angel on the job.

18) Q: As a woman I often wonder whether the *I* doesn't really want to be me and I all at the same time. Is this possible? At times I paint my eyes, arch my brows, paint my face and lips with all sort of cosmetics, trying desperately to form another being, "me." Now, if I believe that "I am I," why do I seek "me" in such a way? You once said some people do this kind of thing because they feel insecure. I believe that many of us want to be ourselves but still do things to imitate others. Is the subconscious in us really saying "I am I," or am I me? — This may seem confusing and maybe even a little ridiculous. Sometimes I feel it takes some stupid or irrelevant or ridiculous question to understand something. Disregard my question if it is out of line!

A: It is not at all out of line. The question concerns all of us, in two ways. First there is the individual mystery: Why was I born at my time as this particular child, in that family and land? In that first respect, the old lady in Boston said, "I accept the universe!" And Emerson remarked, "Gad, she'd better!" Secondly, your question: Does my present form of incarnation suit me as a forward looking *I*? This question faces all of us all the time, though we may not always be keenly aware of it. On account of it, we sometimes try on a different *me*, like a garment, to see tentatively how it might fit. It need not be material like clothes or cosmetics. We may try ourselves at a new job, or a new hobby. It seems to me this is a sign that we are still alive and enterprising. Of course I am only eighty and do not know how a man feels when he has found his final *me* and is ready for the embalmer. An alive religion encourages the quest for the *me* which is right at the given time.

(19)   Q: Is one not likely to become selfcentered in this question of I over me? By selfcentered I mean the boastful *I* bragging and trying to look important in the eyes of other people. Or should the center lie in the *I* who is willing to learn and examine different questions, to better the mind?

       A: The latter. The boastful individual you describe is not aware of the degree to which he is trapped in his own *me* and his "social image." As the religions say, he is in danger of winning the world and losing his soul.

(20)   Q: (1) Since I is soul and conscience, it is therefore a learned faculty. Correct? (2) If so, does this mean man's soul is independent of God?

       A: (1) You seem to have your doubts, and rightly so, as long as you leave me and yourself in the dark as to what you mean by "learned." If you mean our continuous, responsible adjustment of the me to the demands of the I, yes indeed, but in that case you mean the whole man, soul *in* body, "me" *under* conscience. If, however, "learned" should mean patterned from without, adjusted to the formalities that happen to be current in society, that would mean the abdication of conscience, and eventually the loss of soul. As for the demands of the I, that is, of conscience, they are not arbitrary. Conscience does seek the "Will of God" (a mythological expression which, in subsequent chapters we must guard from misinterpretations). Thus for (2), not at all—unless I have misinterpreted your question.

(21)   Q: How can doubt express a certainty of truth?

A: Why do you doubt anything? Can you doubt Christian
Morgenstern's line from *The Great Lalula*: "Simarar kos
malzipempu / sulzuzankunkrei (;)!" Why not? It sounds like
an emphatic assertion, but since we can find nothing but
the music of the syllables, and neither truth nor untruth,
there is no possibility of doubt. Doubt always amounts to
asking; Is this true? Really? I doubt it! Take away the
certainty that there really is truth, and you have no doubt
left.

22)   Q: There will be many obstacles when one is searching
for his truth. One of them is his selfishness. How can one
best deal with this human evil?

A: If the selfishness takes the form of a lazy insistence
that the question asked be answered without ado, start by
placing the question in its proper universe of discourse. In
order to do so, you will probably have to reformulate it.
For instance, many years ago I had a colleague who prided
himself on his skepticism. He threw at me the question:
"How can you really know that $2 + 2 = 4$?" He was a
physicist, and in physics it is quite appropriate to ask how
one can really know whether any mathematical model
corresponds to the physical reality. But place his question
to me into the universe of arithmetic, and it is obvious
that, since we are dealing with whole numbers, not frac-
tions, adding 2 to 2 goes farther than 3 and not as far as 5,
and between 3 and 5 there is nothing but 4. My colleague
"selfishly" stuck to his universe of discourse of physics.

(23)   Q: When searching for truth, what is one to do when he
is attacked by an urgent need to have it at that particular
moment. How can he calm himself?

A: One way is to write out the question, very carefully,
so that it really has a cutting edge. It may then prove to
have several, that is, there may be several questions dis-
guised as one.

Chapter II

THE LANGUAGE OF RELIGION

"As long as we cannot yet inhere in the eternal let us at least reprove our phantasms and expel from the spectacle of our mind such trifling and deceptive plays." Augustine: *De vera religione,* 50,98.

"Only the structure of art, and of mythology in particular, permits us to make God 'talk like a man.'" (57) *"Religious symbols are not susceptible to rationalistic analysis; the ground of their validity is not within the sphere of the objective."* (117) *"Genuine faith is something quite different from belief in the truth of a given mythology."* (125) *"In mythology, the finite form of the historical report affects only the objective sense of the report as intelligence would apprehend it. The truth of the myth, however, insists upon being experienced in the rapt assent to the challenge made by the report. It is a challenge to the whole person and thus transcends the sphere of intelligence."* (127f) Mythology *"may seem to voice objective truth, but this can seem so only to a mind which does not understand what it means to be a self, and which is bound by the objective formulations of its religious symbols."* (239) *"The convincing attack upon the ostensible authority of a mythological story will give to a really free religious life the sense of having been liberated from something painful and confirmed in its confidence in the rights of a living immediacy."* (267) Fritz Medicus: *On Being Human* (Frederick Ungar Publishing Co., New York 1973.)

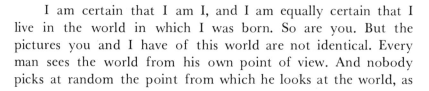

I am certain that I am I, and I am equally certain that I live in the world in which I was born. So are you. But the pictures you and I have of this world are not identical. Every man sees the world from his own point of view. And nobody picks at random the point from which he looks at the world, as he picks an available seat in a half-empty airplane. It is true enough that we do take our stand at will, but within a pattern furnished by family, group, and study. All world pictures are perspectives. And, like a painting or an engraving drawn according to the principles of perspective, a world picture is intelligible only insofar as it offers the possibility of reconstructing the point from which it was seen. Seen from that point, each picture is correct enough. If you look at an elephant from the front you see the trunk but you cannot see the tail; from the rear the tail is visible but maybe not the trunk. It would be silly to say the front view is correct and the rear view wrong, or vice versa.

Men look at the world not only from a point in space but, much more important, from a moment of time. We all live in the same space through which we can travel at will if we can afford the fare. We can go to see how things look from some other spot. We do not all live in the same time when it comes to our world view. Some savages still live in the stone age. Some scientists stand on the threshold of tomorrow. Some philosophers try to follow the advice of Spinoza and see reality from a supertemporal angle, *sub specie aeternitatis,* from the aspect of eternity. Most of our contemporaries live behind the times, at least in most respects. I, for one, have tried to bring myself up to date in philosophy; in physics I missed the boat in 1915, and I take but scant comfort in the stack of books on atomic structure and on galaxies which I have bought for reading in my old age.

Time is of crucial importance in the life of mankind as well as in the life of an individual. In terms of the latter, we can distinguish with Kant the age of childhood when, as he points out, we tend to think dogmatically, the age of adolescence with which comes skepticism, and the age of maturity, to attain which is our lifelong goal. At least it is the goal of some of us. It is an old story. St. Paul says: "When I was a child, I felt as a child, I thought as a child. Now that I have become a man, I have put away the things of a child. We see now through a mirror in an obscure manner, but then face to face." (I Cor. 13:11-12)

(24)   Most of us can never fully put away the things of our

childhood. Man's mind is dogmatic by nature. The world is manifest to us in vivid images, including dream images. And how can we deny that we see or have seen what has appeared to us awake or asleep? How can we completely forget what we were taught as children?

As a student of philosophy I know that I am *I* and that, as *I*, I cannot possibly be thought of as some *It*. Yet, I speak of that mysterious *It*, the soul. On the other hand, as a student who had failed to profit from philosophy I would speak of *It*, my mind, without making the distinction between that aspect of mind which psychology can study objectively and that quite different though vague meaning of the word mind used as a synonym of the word *I*.

Little children sometimes use their own given name as a substitute for I, especially at times when they do not like the fact that, as I, I ought to behave responsibly. My mother used to tell me of an incident which my memory retains only because she told me. When about two and a half I loved to plunge my arm into the sprinkling can my father filled in the morning so that the sun could warm the water. In the last years of the nineteenth century, children in Switzerland were properly dressed, wearing undershirts with long sleeves even in summer. Thus my plunges resulted in a wet undershirt and jersey. Therefore the prohibition: No dipping arms in sprinkling cans! One forenoon, Mama happened to look out the kitchen window right above the can and saw me ready for the forbidden action. She shouted, "Fritzli!" And I looked up at her, calmly stating, "Fritzli does not hear!" What can you expect of a little man who, so he himself informs you, happens to be objectively deaf at the moment? Spank him for lying? She probably did, and I surely deserved it. Yet, the objectification of the *I* comes natural to man. Read *Genesis* 3:12-13: "The man said, 'The woman whom you set at my side, it was she who gave me fruit from the tree; so I ate it.' Then the Lord God said to the woman, 'What ever have you done?' The woman said, 'It was the serpent that misled me, and so I ate it.'"

Blaming another is nothing but a very conspicuous form of objectification of what is not an object. The world confronts man in the form of objects. Why should he not take this form as reality itself? In philosophical jargon, an all pervasive objectivism is called *dogmatism.* It is the natural form of the as yet tender age of the mind when man objectifies everything, selves as well as things. The skeptic will wonder whether there is any such thing as a soul, and whether the gods are anything else but figments of fancy. The skeptic easily overlooks the fact that there are realities like *I* and conscience, and too easily blames the mind of the child and the mentality of man's childhood for trying to acknowledge those facts by means of images like "the soul," and "the Lord God." The skeptic is right when he points out the fanciful nature of the images. But, directed by Plato, should he not substitute concepts for images? Too often, skeptics have mistaken their own word images for objectives; they have not abandoned objectivism, and have become materialists.

Skepticism is a place of rest, not of residence, said Kant. Philosophy all along has endeavored to get beyond skepticism. In the *Phaedo* (61b) Plato has Socrates say that "a poet, in order to be really a poet, should bring forth myths, not concepts." The Greeks, so they said, owed their gods to Homer and Hesiod, the poets. Yet it is precisely Hesiod who started the quest for the concept, as Olof Gigon has pointed out emphatically. (*Der Ursprung der griechischen Philosophie.* Benno Schwabe, Basel 1945; p. 13ff. Compare Kirk and Raven, op. cit., p. 8ff.) Later, Xenophanes said: "If cattle and horses or lions had hands, horses would draw the forms of the gods like horses, cattle like cattle, and they would make their bodies such as they each had themselves." (Kirk and Raven, 169; Diels, fr. 15.) He also said: "Homer and Hesiod have attributed to the gods everything that is a shame and reproach among men, stealing and committing adultery and deceiving each other." (*Ibid.* 168; Diels, fr. 11.) Even earlier than the sixth century's Xenophanes, the writer of *Exodus* may have had in mind a similar objection to anthropomorphism when he put in the mouth of the Lord the Second Commandment (*Ex.* 20:4): "Thou shalt not make any graven image, or any likeness of anything that is in heaven above, or on the earth beneath, or in the water under the earth."

Thus, not only philosophy but religiosity objects to the

natural language of religion, to imagery, because imagery is necessarily objectivistic.

How then are we to speak about religion if we must be skeptical with regard to traditional imagery and yet cannot but retain our natural mind which, like the poet it is, produces images and delights in them? This seems an impass. It is not. The solution is simple: *Keep the images but treat them as what they are, images, not concepts.* It is easy to state so simple a solution; it is not at all easy to adhere to it. Most people are
(25)   much too fond of taking their imagery literally. They are quite unwilling to go beyond Kant's first step. They abhor the second
(26)   step of *skepsis,* because they believe it is the last and will leave them with nothing to cling to, leaving them as what *they* call skeptics, that is, skoffers and deniers. It is high time that schools point out the existence of the third step, which would put such people on the road to maturity. But the establishment seldom goes beyond skepticism and materialism, and its more pusillanimous representatives often give the impression that they prefer to play safe and keep people on the level of dogmatism where images are taken literally. They will put boundary posts around the domain of imagery, markers which say that outside of the domain of imagery the human mind is helpless and remains empty; that the help of revelation alone could fill it. By
(27)   revelation, they seem to mean something like a hot telephone line to heaven. In that manner, they objectify even God and deprive him of divinity. No wonder their offspring lose what they call the faith and what is nothing but beliefs that have proven untenable.* It is the tragedy of our age that schools by and large ignore what has happened in philosophy, the last two centuries. They would have us live before 1776, when David Hume died and Kant was working on his first Critique.

In 1725, Giambattista Vico published his *New Science* in which he pointed out the positive value of imagery. He said that the images are *generi fantastici,* fantastic kind or, paradoxically translated, imaginative concepts. He opened the way to a modern study of mythology which, unlike dogmatism, does not

---

*I have written on "Faith versus Belief," in the *Journal of Religion,* January 1946.

take the images literally nor, like skepticism, try to ignore them. In our century, Ernst Cassirer has written a three volume *Logic of Symbolic Forms.* Between Vico and Cassirer, the way toward understanding images as symbols had been pointed out by Kant, Herder, Fichte, Hegel, and Schelling.

Now let us boldly look at some of the imagery with which most of us have been familiar since childhood. Let us follow the Greeks and admit that it is the poets who create the imagery, and let us remember that the prophets are all poets most of the time, poets who rarely skirt the domain of philosophical concepts. Then we discover at least the sublimity of religious poetry.

Look at the first page of the Bible. The dogmatists or fundamentalists want to take the magnificent picture of creation literally, with the result that they find themselves in conflict with the discoveries of astronomy, geology and biology. They then denounce natural science as a godless and sinful enterprise. In the famous or infamous "monkey trial," at Dayton, Tennessee, in 1927, which made Europe laugh at America, William Jennings Bryan said that, if given the choice between the Bible (meaning the Bible interpreted dogmatically) and science with all its benefits, he would prefer the Bible. His stand was at least consistent. His opponent, Clarence Darrow, formerly an excellent attorney, had not done his homework and argued not like a bold skeptic but like a weak-kneed agnostic. He copped out. Nearly half a century later it still looks as if we had not gone one step further.

But let us really read that first chapter of *Genesis,* with an open mind, and as if we had never read it before. (Students this is an assignment!) Is it not a magnificent picture, more glorious than what Michelangelo painted on the ceiling of the Sistine Chapel? Who can miss the poetry and the beauty of the language (even if, like myself, he must do with a translation). What then is it? Poetry of the greatest! And not "mere poetry" as the barbarians would say, but a chant of praise, as "when the morning stars sang together" (*Job* 38:7). Nowhere is the picture broken by any silly questions about an astronomic and biological time table. It is neither physics nor a tract for or against evolution. It is sheer poetry and deeply religious. It is a glorious expression of faith. It has nothing to do with quibblings about beliefs. Beliefs concern only the intellect. The fundamentalist believer is mostly a weird intellectual, who often lacks real faith altogether. As a self-appointed attorney for God, who is in no need of attorneys, he very easily turns out to be more godless than the agnostic and the unbeliever. At all events, he seems deaf to poetry.

The poet says what the intellectualist cannot tell. Moses says to Jehovah: (*Exodus* 3:13-14): "Behold, when I come to the children of Israel and say to them 'The God of your fathers has sent me to you,' and they say to me 'What is his name?' what shall I say to them. And God said to Moses: 'I shall be who shall be.'" Is there any more powerful, more radiant expression for the reality of uncontroversial authority? In comparison, how weak are the last five words of my question!

John 1:18 has the intellectually quite correct statement: "No one has at any time seen God." Of course, our intellect will want to know why not. The intellectual answer is: Because God's very nature is invisible. So, at that, is the force of gravity, and so is a negative curvature. Such entities do not belong to the domain of things that can be visualized. They are "beyond" the reach of our imagination. For the imagination, they are mysteries. And this is what the imagination must be told, in reply to the intellect's legitimate question: Why has nobody seen God? John answers, after the semicolon of the verse I only half quoted, that the exegesis or interpretation can be found only in the mystery of the Christ: "The only-begotten Son, who is in the bosom of the Father, he has revealed him." The Father is invisible but the incarnate Son visible. And what is the relation between the two? Theology answers: They are not two principles or substances but one. (Our Chapter VII has something to say about such theological statements. For the moment, we will stay with the religious imagination.) The first half of John's verse is an intellectual statement of fact; the second half answers the implied question with an emphatic reminder of the mystery of Christian belief. It does not say God is an invisible reality. In fact, *John* 12:45 and 14:9 has his Christ say that whosoever sees him sees the Father.

The Christian believer clings to this mystery which, for

him, is the last word. For the nonbeliever it is only word, that is, imagery, and he craves a concept. He may turn to different imagery, no less sublime. In *Exodus* 33:18 Moses says to the Lord: "I beseech thee, show me thy glory." And the reply is, 33:19-23: "I will make all my goodness pass before thee. ... Thou canst not see my face, for there shall no man see me and live. ... Behold, ... I will put thee in a cleft of the rock and will cover thee with my hand while I pass by. And I will take away mine hand, and thou shalt see my back parts; but my face shall not be seen." A sublime picture which could be filmed. To be sure, the film would have to resort to thunder and lightning, or to an atomic bomb glare, to hint at the glory of the Lord, since it is invisible. It could do better than the stage technician of Aeschylus whose Prometheus goes down to Tartarus with rumblings and presumably with colophony lightning. But no film can make the invisible visible. The *Exodus* picture is a picture. The intellect can find it quite true. Only God's "back parts" can be seen. That is, *all imagery, once visualized, belongs already to the past.* It is already an articulate image recordable in the memory of believer and unbeliever alike. It is no longer the actual living presence of God.

In our 1970s, many seek the presence of God in their individual experience. They say they have had an extraordinary feeling, and they interpret it as God entering into their minds. "I really felt it all over," they exclaim, and their interpretation stops with that exclamation.

They do not face the fact that every extraordinary experience, like every ordinary one, must be felt in order to be had at all. There is no awareness which does not have an aspect of feeling. With the logic of our enthusiasts every novel experience could be called a presence of God. As for me, I prefer the oldfashioned churchman who summons me to ask myself whether it is really God who inhabits me or the Devil. To be sure it is our intellect which distinguishes between the two, but without the distinction feelings have no truth value. They come and go like dissolving spring clouds. If you banish all thinking you open the door to the Devil. Mephistopheles himself tells you, "go ahead and despise reason and science, then I have already an absolute hold on you" (Goethe: *Faust,* I, lines 1851/5). In order to retain a hold on ourselves we need certainty, and when we want to understand the truths conveyed by religion we need philosophical certainty, not scientific constructions.

The religious poet knows (or feels at least) that the object to which his images seem to point is a mystery. The schoolish mind may call it an illusion as Freud did, not knowing that the so-called First Cause is not an object and is beyond the scope of science. If such a mind could be made to pause and, faced with the question of a first ground, would ask "Just exactly what do I mean?" it might discover that what is meant could be an act (28) instead of a fact, as Fichte pointed out (I,8), in 1794. A little later that same year Fichte also indicated the difficulty most of us encounter when trying to think philosophically, that is, plainly, especially about ourselves and our religious foundations. He wrote: "Most people could be more easily induced to take themselves for a piece of lava in the moon, than for an I. . . . Thus we posit our *I* outside of ourselves as a thing existing (who knows how?) without any action on our part. And this thing is supposed to be affected by some other thing, somewhat in the manner in which a magnet affects a piece of iron." (I,175)

It is this quite natural objectivistic thinking, or half-thinking, which causes people to turn religious reality into a set of unintelligible objects, and which prevents an adequate understanding of that reality and sometimes even an alive and personal feeling for it.

This is the basic problem of our whole enterprise here. There is no quick remedy. You, as a true student, must keep working at it. You must educate or reeducate yourself, so that you can take not only the second but the third step of Kant.

Student Questions

(24) Q: I imagine that, through your kind of instruction, you can help more people than many a "called" preacher. There may be more "Christians" sitting at home than in churches. You have stated that you do not belong to any particular denomination. Why? Did not your first feelings or beliefs start in some church?

A: Ours was not a churchgoing family. Father and grand-
mother never attended except for a wedding or funeral.
Mother went once or twice a month. But she did not teach
us any formal beliefs. Through her I came to see the
beauty of the stars, and more particularly of plants and
small animals, like song birds, and ants and butterflies, and
a feeling for the "dear God" who let them be and grow. I
cannot remember any use of ecclesiastic terminology, not
even of the word Creator. While in grade school I was sent
to Sunday school, where I became fond of Biblical history,
especially of the Old Testament. But we did not read the
Bible, and only at college level did I discover a writer like
St. Paul, whom I loathed. It is through the study of
philosophy that I began to take theological doctrines
seriously to the point of wanting to know what kind of
truth they could convey.—What I cannot explain at all is
the fact that, at seventeen and eighteen, I became the only
regular churchgoer of the family and rarely missed a
Sunday. Owing to some inner deficiency I may have needed
a feeling of security more personal than what good home
life provided. More personal also than the weekly instruction before my confirmation at sixteen. Palm Sunday 1910
I found that the eucharistic wine (protestant white wine!)
tasted like a good country wine, and the cubic inch of
bread like wholesome peasant bread. I do not know what
heavenly flavor I had anticipated. I attended the instruction
with considerable boredom. It was nothing but ethics, the
state church of Bern and of the other protestant cantons in
Switzerland being, at that time, "liberal" or, in American
terms, Unitarian. The instruction carefully bypassed all
Christology. In my view Unitarians are not Christians.
Christian theology is trinitarian. As for your second question, maybe this book tells you why I cannot belong to
any denominational religion.

(25) Q: Is it possible that a schizophrenic's belief, in his
fantasy life, is his own religion, and if so can a religious
belief be compared to living in a schizophrenic state of
mind?

A: At least you say "compared," not "is." The latter
would be against logic. If it is true that your schizophrenic's beliefs are his religion ("All SB are R") what
follows logically is only that this is the case of *his* religion
but not of everybody's ("Some R is SB," and not "All R is
SB").

Though many religionists would not say with
Augustine that God is the truth, yet religion means to
proclaim truth. Therefore, you move away from the reality
of religion, and not toward it, when you try to understand
it in psychological or psychiatric terms. It is not the task of
the psychologist and psychiatrist to ascertain whether and
why the notions in the mind of his patient are true; what
interests psychology and psychiatry is the way such notions
work in that mind. By means of psychology, you may
come to better understand the particular religionist but not
his religion. The latter requires adequate philosophical
terms.

(26)   Q: There are many atheists in the world. These people
truly believe that there is no supreme being, "God." How
can they live from day to day without something that can
account for their very existence? Isn't it necessary for them
to have "faith"? I feel you have to have something or
someone to hook faith on to. ???? Can you explain?

A: The atheist has faith in truth. How else could he say
with conviction there *is* no God? Sometimes a negative
truth is very comforting, for instance when the physician
says to the patient: There is no cancer! It is the atheist's
faith in truth which makes him reject an untenable con-
ception of God. Like the believer in that kind of a god, the
atheist assumes it is the only kind. In Nietzsche's *Zarathustra* (Part IV, "Out of Service") after the death of God
the last Pope, now out of service, comes into the wilderness
to seek "the most pious among those who do not believe in
God" and finds him, Zarathustra, who says: "There is good
taste in piety too; and it was taste which finally said, 'away
with that kind of a god'." And the last Pope replies: "What
do I hear! Oh, Zarathustra, you are more pious than you

believe, having your kind of unbelief! Is it not your very piety which no longer permits you to believe in god?"

What about the faith of the Marxists? They believe in the inexorable coming of world communism and therefore do not believe in any kind of God who could stop it, in any divine personage who could desire to change events. They believe in Fate. That is "something to hook on to," as you put it. So you are quite right. What I'd like to know is what your string of question marks stand for.

As for the skeptic, he has faith in the truth so remote from man, so hidden, that only utter conceit could make one believe he could reach the truth.

(27) Q: A prevalent doctrine in the Catholic Church is that of Christ's promise to Peter and his successors of freedom from all blemish of error in their teachings. How do you interpret this pronouncement by Jesus Christ?

A: I cannot interpret what I cannot find. The closest (and only) verses pointing to the direction of such a doctrine are Matthew 16:19 "And I will give thee the keys of the kingdom of heaven; and whatever thou shalt bind on earth shall be bound in heaven, and whatever thou shalt loose on earth shall be loosed in heaven"; and *Matthew* 18:18 which, however, is addressed to all the disciples. To bind and to loose seems to mean legal decisions such as absolution or anathema. It does not say freedom of error in teaching. Nor does it establish any apostolic succession of Peter, which was unnecessary according to *Matthew* 24:34, "this generation will not pass away till all these things have been accomplished." (I am quoting the translation from the Vulgate published by the St. Anthony Guild Press, Paterson, N.J. 1941.)

(28) Q: What does Fichte mean by "an act instead of a fact"?

A: In 1792, in his *Review of Aenesidemus* (I,8) Fichte wrote that, in order to establish a first principle of all philosophy, one must not make the erroneous assumption that "one ought to start from a fact. To be sure, what is needed is a real, not a merely formal principle. But that need not be a fact (Tatsache) it can be an act (Tathandlung) instead." The distinction between act and fact goes back to Aristotle's distinction between acting (práttein) and being acted upon (páthein). However, for Aristotle only God is pure act and nothing else. Fichte found pure act in the *I*. In Chapter I we said: Nobody can be I for me. And I am I only insofar as I posit myself (to use Fichte's expression), that is, insofar as I enact my freedom. I cannot be coerced by anybody nor by any circumstances into discovering that I am I. What is needed is my active curiosity, my own question: "What do I mean when I say 'I' and by that word refer to myself?" If I do so ask, and find that I am indeed I, this asking and finding can be called a fact, the fact that I did ask and find. This fact is the consequence of my act. In other words, my act results in the psychological fact, but the latter cannot be transformed back into the spontaneous act. The bullet does not return into the gun. The movement from cause to effect is not reversible. (The last two sentences deal with factual examples, with things, not selves.)

As you should know by now, nobody can make you see or can show you that you *are* what you call (your) *I*. Only you yourself can do it, by your own act. As long as you have not grasped this, the door of philosophy is locked for you. And that means that you are restricted to Kant's first two steps, that is, either you must, like a child, take religion as just stories no matter how sincerely believed, or else you must join the skeptic and declare that the stories of religion are nothing but fairy tales. If you do not like that alternative, study our Chapter I again, in order to go beyond both, the child and the skeptic.

Chapter III

THE CHARM OF INTOXICATION AND THE CHALLENGE OF SOBER THOUGHT

Heraclitus said:

> "*A man when he is drunk is led by an immature boy, stumbling and not knowing where he goes.*" (Diels, fragment 117. Kirk and Raven: *The Presocratic Philosophers*, page 205)

> "*They vainly purify themselves of blood-guilt by defiling themselves with blood, as though one who had stepped into mud were to wash with mud.*" (Diels, fr. 5; K & R 211)

> "*The secret rites practised among men are celebrated in an unholy manner.*" (Diels, fr. 14; K & R 211)

> "*If it were not to Dionysus that they made the procession and sung the hymn to the shameful parts, the deed would be most shameless.*" (Diels, fr. 15; K & R 211)

> "*Although the Logos is common, the many live as though they had a private understanding.*" (Diels, fr. 2; K & R 188)

> "*And they were all filled with the Holy Ghost, and began to speak with other tongues.*" — "*And they were all amazed and perplexed, saying to one another, 'What does this mean?' But others said in mockery, 'They are full of new wine.'*" *Acts* 2:4 and 12-13.

> "*Tongues are intended as a sign, not to believers, but to unbelievers; whereas prophecies not to unbelievers but to believers. Therefore, if the whole church be assembled together and, while all are speaking with tongues, there should come in uninstructed persons or unbelievers, will they not say that you are mad? — If anyone speaks in a tongue, let it be by twos or at most by threes, and let them speak in turn, and let one interpret.*" *I Cor.* 14:22-23 and 27.

(29)

"The true is the bacchanalian giddiness, where not a soul is sober; and because every member, as soon as it stands apart, immediately dissolves, the frenzy turns out to be a state of transparent unbroken calm." (Werke II,37, Berlin 1832: *"Das Wahre ist so der bacchantische Taumel, an dem kein Glied nicht trunken ist, und weil jedes, indem es sich absondert, ebenso unmittelbar sich auflöst, ist er eben so die durchsichtige und einfache Ruhe."*) Hegel: *Phenomenology of Mind*

"Morality is a matter of changing the chemical structure of the body." Nietzsche (Gross- und Kleinoktavausgabe XIV, 318)

◆——◆——◆

Chemically, life is a continuous and continuously changing intoxication. We call certain influences from without toxic. But the body itself produces all kinds of chemical compounds as long as there is life. We call them normal when they enhance life, and abnormal when they hinder it. Everybody knows that adrenalin puts the body in fighting trim. And even Archie Bunker knows that "them hormones" make a guy dangerous to a girl's virtue. So does alcohol, if we are to believe the Women's Christian Temperance Union. The good ladies did not know how close their belief was to Nietzsche's view. Maybe they should have replaced their preachers with chemists, in order to redeem the errant males.

Nevertheless, biochemistry cannot tell the whole story, since chemical analysis would tell us that there is nothing to the big centerfold pictures of Playboy but paper and the ingredients of fleshtone pigments. It is the psychological effect of the pictures which worries the moralist. (The business managers of Playboy may be worried about Danish competition, which is another case of ideas moving the world.) For we are all moved by ideas, olfactory, visual, auditive or intellectual. Indeed, we can become intoxicated with ideas.

Primitive man seeks such intoxication quite frankly. A war dance surely increases the flow of adrenalin. And the idea that a president in the flesh actually shook your hand is supposed to make you vote his ticket, and his opponent risks a sore hand for the same magic power of body over mind.

It is sad that the materialism of the temperance ladies

makes them forget that they themselves can become quite intemperate in imbibing ideas. Every kind of fanaticism is a case of mental intoxication. Just as an overdose of alcohol may make your legs wobbly and your navigation unsteady, so can an excess of unchecked ideas deprive you of sober judgment.

Now we need not deny the touch of charm often found in slight tipsiness. I am not thinking so much of the mind of the tippler, as of his social image. He has turned out to be a jolly good fellow. In the gay days of Prohibition, H. L. Mencken ventured to say that the nation would be much better off, socially and politically, if everybody all the time could be "slightly stewed"—a notion which our rulers should ponder!

The question, of course, is how slight is slightly. How much ideational intoxication and indoctrination can a given society stand? When does intoxication turn into addiction? And when does indoctrination become totalitarianism?

Not only can we get drunk on ideas, we can become ideational drunkards. And, as far as our chosen topic is concerned, man can most certainly get drunk on religion. Examples need not be borrowed from past times, like an *auto-da-fe*, (i.e., an act of faith, a verdict pronounced by the Inquisition), nor from distant lands, like Stalinist purges of Marxist faith. We can stay right on campus and contemplate our own, though very modest, ideational intemperance which has permitted legislative decisions to deviate from the principle of separation of church and state. (I am realistic enough to know that the principle cannot be adhered to rigoristically.)

My concern is not political, it is philosophical. And my question is whether religion can remain religious if it gives in to ideational intemperance. And what must worry us more is the question whether any religion, as soon as "organized," does not automatically become doctrinaire, that is, intemperate and tipsy in the evaluation of its basic ideas.

Ideas cannot be picked up from the ground, like rocks from the moon. They are the products of long historical development, and their formulations, down to their very words, are historically conditioned, by social custom and also by bold innovators.

Ideas do not tumble gracefully from the sky like snow-flakes. They may start as hunches in "inspired" minds. And such

(30) minds then struggle for definitions, often for a long time and painfully, though once in a while they find the right words which give body to the idea, in a flash. I would not object to Plato when he says we get our ideas from heaven. In fact, their origin is precisely what will concern us in subsequent chapters. My objection is to the generalization of the fact that, once in a while, an idea does not start as a mere hunch but arises in a mind fullbodied, clad in so many precise words. (When Zeus desired a radical cure of his headache and asked Hephaistos, the smith, to hit the divine forehead with a sledgehammer, Athena sprang forth fullgrown, and with helmet and spear.) For the moment, let us fully agree with Plato, that ideas come from heaven. Nevertheless their wording is terrestial, not celestial. Furthermore, the wording of religious ideas is poetical, not prosaic; imaginative, not formally conceptual, though it may skirt the conceptual domain.

(31) In short, I object to the common prosaic notion of revelation, according to which heaven sends us trans-space radiograms, not in any code (like the golden Book of Mormon) but fully spelled out in plain English, and to be taken literally. This is a very unrealistic notion, because it flatly ignores the historical circumstances of the receiving set or sets, which are human minds at a definite moment of time, and under definite cultural conditions.

(32) If revelations were spelled out messages they would have to be accepted in slavish submission, as flat orders from a celestial potentate. It would be insubordination not only to question them but even to expect to understand them. Reason would have to be squelched. In fact, reason would be quite superfluous, and a quick and retentive memory would be the appropriate endowment of a religious man. And our unsquelchable reason will ask, would it not be best for man to be endowed with a religious instinct which would make him obey automatically whatever heaven wants. Such an instinct would have prevented Adam's Fall.

(33) Why do we need reason at all? And what has reason to do with religion? Or, rather, does religion by any chance turn irreligious without the service of reason? These are questions to be dealt with in the next chapters.

For the moment, let us grant the fact that religious intoxication has its charm, at least for minds not eager to mature. Everything is written down and spelled out in the sacred books, and all man has to do is follow orders. The chief, in fact the only human virtue, as Hitler taught, is obedience. To be sure, that raises the awkward problem of dissent. But human imagination can readily cope with that. It will dream up tiger cages, Siberian lumber camps, or places like Dachau and Auschwitz, or at least imagine the Falkland Islands as a place for dissenters. A forward questioner might ask whether imaginative solutions are Christian or, more generally speaking, religious in any sense.

Enough about the charm of tipsy imagination. But what about addiction? The addict is inclined to go the same round, over and over again. He cannot get out of his magic circle. He has lost the critical ability to call a stop. And, similar to the spell of alcohol on the alcoholic, ideas have a way of keeping their victims spellbound. Take the "domino theory" about communist aggression in southeast Asia. Its spell led us deeper and deeper into the mess. Nobody in authority seemed to wonder whether a different theory might not explain, and explain better, the events in North Vietnam. For instance, the theory of nationalism. Suppose the Vietnamese want to rule themselves and want to get rid of *all* foreign intrusion. When Ho Chi Minh got rid of the French, he did not replace them with the Chinese. He did need outside help and approached us and we turned him down. Then he found help from Russia and China, communist powers. He, too, was a communist. And that fearsome word kept us spellbound, as if intoxicated.

Unfortunately, our political jags are not without ties to our religious spells. A hundred years ago, when the European powers still carried "the white man's burden" and when our country was only on its way to becoming the greatest power, it was natural (though not excusable) that white people on both sides of the Atlantic looked down upon Asians and Africans. The whites were in the safe possession of "the true religion," and part of their burden was the conversion of black and brown and yellow people. In their conceit, they forgot an earlier wave of world mission, the one which had brought large sections of Asia and Africa into the "true faith" of Islam. And now we are faced with a third and even bigger wave of missionary enterprise supported by the firm conviction that the newer and "truer" religion of Marxism will yet embrace the whole world. Of

(34) course, it is a godless religion, but that makes it all the stronger. And this, so it would seem, scares many of our compatriots more than the threat to the nineteenth century type of catch-as-catch-can capitalism. We have replaced the latter with an economic system which American capitalists of a hundred years ago would have called rank socialism. True, we do not like state ownership of the means of production. But are we ready to go to war about it? And is not our policy of containment and our long warfare in Vietnam (overt till recently and now covert) secretly a religious rather than an economic war? Surely, if the Third World War should come and still leave a little time for explanations, many of our church people would justify it as the war against the godless.

By now, it would seem obvious that wars accomplish nothing and bring only misery. And religious wars are outright ridiculous. Religious problems must be thought out, not fought about. Thought, however, requires sacrifice in the form of a willingness to reconsider and re-evaluate old ideas. This is the

(35) challenge to the true student whose task it is to rediscover and reformulate the Logos, the meaning of things. Study unites us in common cause. But the many who loathe study live as if understanding were a private affair of sheer taste and intoxica-

(36) tion. The student finds his calm in the exciting bacchanal of the ideas.

Student Questions

(29) **Q:**   What does Hegel mean by the giddiness of the true?

A: To become aware of anything (a pleasure, a pain, the sight of beauty, or of ugliness, a fair act or a foul, a convincing truth or a dubious assertion) means to be fascinated by it, for the moment. The intoxicating moment of discovery may soon give way to the hangover of doubt. And, like a drinking man who quite willingly drifts on the billows of intoxication yet tells himself he must and can keep a level head, we may simultaneously experience our assent to the novel awareness and our sobering question as to the value of whatever we experience. If the experience that comes to us looks definitely true, we are not always satisfied with its intoxicating convincingness but would also like to have a sober confirmation. What comes is *definitely* so, our experience tells us; and yet the question also comes: Is it *truly* so? Thus we take our stand with the experience (how could we help it?) and also with the possible doubt. In a bacchanal, the really drunken ones will reel into the bushes and pass out, and some who are nearly drunk may get a hold of themselves and leave the revelry. The party either dissolves or breaks up. Similarly, the appearance of what is true may take the form of a dogma and, like an undertow, wash some of us out into the billowing sea of irresponsibility, or else the reveler may be sobered by his doubts, and quit. If he merely quits he is a spoilsport and, for him, the apparent truth is meaningless and immediately dissolves. Yet if he does not quit the game but only its first fascination and now takes his doubts seriously, not standing apart from the apparent truth but looking for its true core and finding it, then the doubt is dissolved though not immediately. The doubt belongs to the truth and brings it into clear focus. Then, what seemed a drunken reel, back and forth between apparent truth and doubt, is resolved in an unbroken transparent calm.

Oh, yes, you are quite right in now asking for an explanation of my explanation. Why not explain it yourself? Simply take the case in which something appeared convincingly true to you, and then take your concomitant doubt seriously and watch how the solution resolves the frenzy into lucid calm, a calm which would not have come without the frenzy. The proof cannot be given in the abstract. You must pick an example of your own experience and boldly keep watching what happens in your mind. I say, watch! Do not queer the game with an academic endeavor to prove Hegel right. He also watched and reported. He had no dogma to defend.

(30) Q: When an idea comes to a person full-grown can this be considered to be a revelation?

A: It certainly reveals a reality not of our deliberate making. In order to have an academic word for it, call it at least the reality of the subconscious. In March and April of 1957, during a seminar on the subconscious, at the School of Psychiatry in Washington, Martin Buber pointed out that, at times, the subconscious (das Unbewusste) "leads to a half-articulate exclamation, which is what no prepared and already available word can do. In such a case, the voice becomes the immediate instrument of the subconscious." (*Nachlese*, p. 182. Verlag Lambert Schneider, Heidelberg 1965.) Your "full-grown idea" makes use of available words but it is their composition which corresponds to the half-articulate manifestation of reality. Now, if you want to replace such cautious words as reality or the subconscious by mythological terms and say that a revelation comes from God, intellectual conscience speaks up and asks whether it truly comes from God or rather from the Devil. And if you define revelation as what comes from God, full-grown, then the answer to your question is: Not always! Reason demands that we study case by case. And the opinions differ. Joan of Arc took the voices she heard at Angelus time seriously, as explicit orders, but the ecclesiastic court of Rouen told her they were from the Devil, and she was burned. (Read George Bernard Shaw's *Saint Joan*, and also Shaw's preface.) Bernadette Soubirou testified that, in 1858, she repeatedly saw "the beautiful lady" in the grotto at Lourdes, but the church at first told her it was just an illusion and then, reversing itself, that it must have been the Blessed Virgin. (Read Franz Werfel's *The Song of Bernadette*, The Viking Press, N.Y., 1943). The one who has visions or hears voices cannot but testify to the fact. But the intellect, either of the visionary himself or of others, steps in and tries to distinguish between illusion and revelation.

(31) Q: In general, organized religion has been rather dogmatic
in its pronouncements. For this reason it has been rejected
by many philosophers who pride themselves on being
rational. Yet cannot these rational men fall into the same
trap of dogmatism and inflexibility? If so, can dogmatic
reason be much better than blind religious beliefs?

      A: If we take the word reason to mean the perpetual
readiness to reexamine every formulation, even the most
lucid sentences found in philosophy, then the phrase "dogmatic reason" is a contradiction in terms. But let us not
quibble about words. What you are talking about is the
dogmatism inherent in any argumentation which uncritically assumes that formally correct sentences can exhaustively
express truth. Such an assumption is not better but worse
than blind belief which at least admits mystery.

(32) Q: I say I believe in God; I have faith in God. Can it be
that really I mean that I believe and have faith in my ideas.
Isn't God a word we stamp on our ideas?

      A: Of course it is a word. The question is what is meant
by it in a given context and in the individual mind. For
many, "God" means a celestial dictator. For others it
means what the muezzin's call for prayer says: "Allah is
merciful!" And Augustine says that, at the very least, God
is truth, the truth which dwells in the inner man. The
writer of *Acts* (17:28) says, "in him we live and move and
have our being." In contrast, a man who knows only the
superstitious meaning of the word and has discovered the
superstition, rightly says God is dead. (See note 3.)

(33) Q: "Does religion by any chance turn irreligious without
the service of reason?" If I am not mistaken, many
religions have tried to do away with reason by indoctrinat-
ing their followers to stop at ostensibly final formulations
thought up perhaps hundreds of years ago. This is not what
religion is all about. Reason demands private thought on
ideas produced by you alone. Therefore, if a person joins a

religion, doesn't he miss out on Kant's third step of
maturity? (Last paragraph of Chapter I.)

A: Reason (or conscience) does indeed demand that we
follow the example of Israel, that wrestler with God
(*Genesis* 32:28), and valiantly struggle till blessed with
understanding. However, there has to be something to be
understood. There can be no thought without a topic. You
cannot wrestle in private, without an antagonist. Thought is
truly private, but you need something to think about, and
something that seems to make sense. Worthwhile ideas are
not "produced by you alone"; they are the result of your
valiant wrestling with problems which confront you, standing in your way like the man before Jacob. You are quite
right, only having wrestled with a problem can you be
blessed with a solution. And, like the great scientists, you
may see a problem nobody has yet seen. Nevertheless you
find it, you do not produce it from nothing.

Now as for "joining" a religion, why would anyone do
that unless he saw some promise in it, be it even as little as
a bit of comfort. The student, of course, seeks more; he
seeks truth. And, knowing that truth comes to him only in
private, he will not expect any religion to offer it to him
ready made, in a capsule to be swallowed without chewing.
It is precisely because the student has taken the second,
skeptical step beyond the first which is dogmatic, and
because he is desirous to take the third, toward a "mature,
manly judgment," that he would "join" an enterprise which
offers some promise.

(34) Q: "Marxism is a godless religion, but that makes it all
the stronger." I cannot understand how a religion without
God can be strong. Please explain.

A: When confronted with a task, man is often tempted to
say, "let George do it!" And he may be inclined to put
God in the shoes of George. Every superstitious prayer does
just that, turning God into a convenient fix-it man. Such a
temptation cannot face a man who has no God and who,
therefore, must either dodge the task or do it himself. Marx

summoned the proletarians to help themselves. Socialism and the Marxist paradise of a classless society will not come without the dedicated effort of Marxist believers. Their eschatological belief that that blessed state of things will surely come gives them the strength of perseverance but does not cancel out, fatalistically, the inexorable need for human effort. Marxists do not believe in fairy godmothers.

Buddhism similarly appeals to man's own efforts. Christianity injects another thought, the notion of Grace (found already in Judaism). No matter how well we do our work, we can never boast that it is done by our own merit alone. "Man cannot save himself," may sound dogmatic. But we are never completely masters of our circumstances, and if we succeed we do so "by the Grace of God." This may be what is on your mind. A more secular phrase would be "by luck." But that really explains nothing, since it means "by happenstance." Give it a mythological name, and you have fickle Fortune. Turn the feminine into a masculine and you wind up with an arbitrary God who, like a crooked croupier, can slow down the roulette wheel and make the ball stop on the number of his favorites. Then Grace has vanished. In truth, however, far from being the opposite of justice, Grace is its complement. An arbitrary God can furnish neither Justice nor Grace, and his religion gives no strength. In contrast to such a religion, any form of determinism is stronger.

(35) Q: In class you said: "When philosophy starts turning out dogmas it stops being philosophy." I thought dogmas were part of philosophy. Every religion has dogmas often passed down through the centuries. Does their re-evaluation break them down so that the thought remains a part of philosophy?

      A: "Yes" would do for a one-word answer. However, your difficulty seems to spring from not distinguishing between dogma and doctrine. The latter is a teaching device, the former is "of the faith" (de fide). Church councils write definitions in an endeavor to express in clear words what the dogma means. But formulations bear the mark of their time, and a new time demands still clearer expressions based on deeper philosophical insight. Hence my yes. As to whether churches recognize this relation between religion and philosophy, that depends on the historical circumstances, and on the level a culture has reached. To be sure, the two words, Greek *dogma* and Latin *doctrina,* originally mean the same thing, simply "what is being taught." But in the current meaning, what is taught is not necessarily true; there are erroneous doctrines. In the strict sense of ecclesiastic dogma, there can be no error in dogma. For instance, the Christian dogma that the godhead is triune (Father, Son, and Holy Ghost) claims a truth independent of any teaching; the ancient Hebrews were not taught about the Holy Trinity except maybe by hints such as the *three* angels who visited Abraham. Similarly the multiplication table is timelessly true and was true long before men learned to add, subtract, multiply and divide. True enough, in time the dogmas of the church are re-evaluated. New ecumenic councils write new "definitions," in an endeavor to make the truth of a dogma clearer. Your question then is: Does such clarification eventually peel off all obscurities of former formulations? And is what is left a philosophical truth of interdenominational and inter-faith dignity? Many a philosopher may say yes. But others, especially churchmen, teach that the truth of dogma is beyond the reach of philosophy and must come to man, if at all, in the form of revelation.

It all depends on what you mean by revelation. If you have been indoctrinated and made to believe that the word "I" designates nothing but a mind, that is, a complex mental phenomenon reported by the individual afflicted by a mind, you might as well believe that you are a piece of lava on the moon, as Fichte put it in 1794. If then some book or teacher induced you to ask: "What do I mean when I say I?" and if it comes to you like a flash that "I means that I am I for myself alone, and nobody can be I for me," then you may well be inclined to call this insight a revelation. *Velum* means a veil; and indeed the veil of your indoctrination has been lifted and you clearly see the truth. And considering that you might not have come across that book or that teacher, you may feel like saying, "Thank God for my having been led to the insight!" Augustine said: "Oh, eternal truth, true love, beloved eternity, thou art my God." (Conf. VII,x,16.)

On the other hand, if by revelation you do not mean any better understanding of yourself but some strange piece of information about entities entirely foreign to you, then it has a magical dignity impenetrable to philosophy. Philosophy has no dogmas. And its doctrines remain unphilosophical as long as they are not understood in their relevance for the student.

(36) Q: Most of the organized religions differ in at least some small way in their teachings about God. There can be only one right way. (a) Then, are the people who do not follow this way lost? (b) A person who believes in his religion has found the truth for him. (c) He has met the challenge of truth. (d) I see no reason to condemn anyone for their religious beliefs. (e)

A: (a) If you deal with whole numbers and add two and two, there is only one result, four. Three would be too little and five too much. But are religious doctrines as simple as arithmetic? When Jews and Moslems say God is One, Christians agree. How could they disagree? But when Christians speak of the trinity and specifically of the incarnate Son, Jews and Moslems consider the doctrine of an incarnate God blasphemic. (b) Dogmatically, each side says the other is lost. They are both lost to further inquiry. And they are lost formally, since neither is clearly aware that religious language is often poetic at decisive points. Therefore to say there can be only one way is much like saying there is only one poem, or there is only one language. Or only one view of an elephant, either from the front where you cannot see the tail or from the rear where you may not see the trunk. Religious views are perspectives, sights from some specific historical standpoint.

You are really lost (lost to humanity) if you cannot see the other's point of view. Thus you are quite right in saying a believer "has found the truth for him." (c) However you forget your previous principle that there are not two truths, but one. Your religionist does not forget that, and he says that what is true for him must also be true for everybody concerned with truth. So he starts his missionarizing in all seriousness. For "he has met the challenge of truth." (d) Quite so. But he now has stopped at a point where he should have followed that challenge further. And should he not be condemned for that? (e) You can condemn for various reasons. (1) Because you yourself do not like it. (2) Because it is illegal. And indeed in our country you are legally at liberty to embrace any religious belief that appeals to you. (3) Because it is a tort to somebody. For instance, a belief that men are by nature superior to women is a tort to all women, even to those who are willing to do the bidding of their husband as their lord and master. Thus, to declare that religious beliefs are a mere matter of individual whim is a tort, first to all serious religions, and second to the rational dignity of man. As serious students we ought to condemn such a declaration as a perversion of the interrelation of religion and reason. Religion cannot say, "to hell with all truth." That would be an expression of irreligion.

Chapter IV

THE AUTHORITY OF IDEAS

"I hope God will grant that I may capably answer you, or rather that you, being inwardly taught by that very truth which is the highest teacher of all, will answer yourself." Augustine: *De libero arbirtrio,* II,ii,4.

"If there is anything higher, then that is God; if not, the truth itself is already God." Augustine: ib. II,xv,39.

"Oh, eternal truth, and true love, and beloved eternity, you are my God!" Augustine: *Confessions,* VII,x,16.

"The truth does not come to itself by argument but it is what those who argue desire." Augustine: *De vera religione,* 39,72.

"The meaning of Augustine's dictum that God is truth becomes clear; if a man's experiencing of a situation in which he stands (whatever it may be) is fully adequate to the reality of the situation in its depths, then in that experience he knows God" (257). "Truth in its depths, hidden from one who has abandoned himself to baseness, demands the whole man. It claims him as one who stands superior to the events in the objective world and above the concerns by which this world is agitated" (222). "The proposition that the certainty of God has its origin in one's own experience, and is therefore immanent, requires a complement which secures the rights of transcendence" (276f). Fritz Medicus: *On Being Human* (Frederick Ungar Publishing Co., New York 1973.)

◆—◆—◆

When you lie down to sleep, you may make plans for tomorrow's activities. You cannot plan the night's dreams. Dreams come upon you unplanned and uncalled for. Likewise, some ideas come upon us without any obvious reason. Some we call hunches. Other ideas come through teaching and reading, or through deliberate personal observation of the world around us. All ideas exert a spell upon us, at least for the moment. Some, like most of the ideas of Archie Bunker, are fixed. They may have the power of obsessions. This is why Archie feels he is always right.

People who are hungry for power implant as best as they can such obsessive ideas in the minds of their fellow men. Just look at the tedious endeavors of TV advertising. Hitler was a past-master of ideational propaganda. He pointed out, in his advertising textbook, *Mein Kampf,* that ideas need not be true; even the most obviously false idea, if repeated frequently enough, and in the tone of conviction, will eventually stick in people's minds as if it were undubitably true.

(37) Some deluded and scared champions of religion have done unspeakable damage to religiosity by presenting religious doctrines as if perpetual repetition could make a doctrine convincing. Their delusion lies in their own ignorance. What they know is the wording of the doctrines, but they do not know that doctrines are the result of some honest, though at times untutored endeavor to give intellectual expression to religious feelings. The life of a doctrine must be rediscovered by an historical study of the minds who formulated it. Merely to call such minds inspired authorities does not help. You must study the way in which they arrived at their doctrine. You may own twenty volumes written by St. Augustine but, when confronted with a theological query, it does you no good to lay your hand on the books and have your *mouth* repeat the invocation, "Dear St. Augustine, help!" You must bend your *mind* upon the content of the specific book which deals with your particular problem. The church is quite right in saying that the saints will help, but you must make the right approach, in the spirit of the specific question. Otherwise the saint will remain mute, and his writings a book with seven seals. Religious ideas demand to be taken for ideas rather than magical incantations. And ideas present themselves as being true, even if they are patently false. We are endowed with our intellect for a purpose. We must ask: "Is this true? And just how true?"

So far I have used the word idea in the sense in which it is ordinarily used. In current parlance (and in the mind of

Berkeley) idea means anything in the mind, a feeling, an intention, a hunch, an image, a doctrine, and sometimes even a clear cut concept. Plato called all such mental contents opinions, which indeed they are. He emphasized that there is a difference between an opinion (*dóxa*) and a demonstrable truth, and it was the latter he called an *idéa*. This noun cames from the verb *ideîn*, to see. If I do see anything, the view or *sight* I have is quite literally what the word idea means. However, Plato uses the word only for a meaning that is provable, not for a mere image that hovers in my memory as an opinion. From here on, I shall use the word in Plato's sense.

Here, of course, we stand at the point where the way bifurcates. Some minds do not seek proof. For a young infant a thing is demonstrably real if he can put his fingers upon it or preferably put it in his mouth. All the evidence he has is sense evidence. Later, he finds proof in authority, "mother said," or "teacher told us," or prefereably though still a little later "the gang says." And when such a mind finds that human authorities are not always trustworthy, he will try to locate a superhuman authority which he is likely to call God, not knowing what he is saying. (We shall soon see what divine authority is, in truth.)

(38) If the authority-ridden mind should have spells of inquisitiveness, he will be put down by the prospect of penalties for insubordination. Might is right. And once he learns this lesson he will become a good organization man and do what he is told, or at least furnish a fair facsimile of submissiveness. In the Swiss army which, from 1914 to 1918, often heavily taxed our patience with waiting and doing nothing, the boys used to ask, "What is the main thing you learn in military life?" and they would answer, "To stand around in a lively manner."

The authoritarian mind finds his reward when he himself moves up among the authorities. Archie Bunker is quite a boss over his three fellow workers. And should they fail him he can always boss Edith, his wife.

(39) To ask questions, and especially to question the establishment, appears as a rather frightening mental aberration to the authoritarian mind. Thus, if I spoke of a bifurcation of roads, do not draw the picture of a Y, but rather a K without the leg that supports the deviating offshoot. For the authoritarian, there

is no real support of the deviation, and the age of adolescence appears as an age of delinquency, which, of course, it is if the adolescent does not take Kant's third step, into maturity supported by study.

Yet the questions stare us in the face. Depict them as offshoots from the upright trunk of the K, but do not forget that the trunk of the tree depends on the roots, and if you look at the roots, they are a whole system of offshoots, seeking nourishment in all directions. So of course are the branches which seek light. Thus, the drawing of a tree's roots, trunk and branches would better illustrate a healthy mind than would the vertical line of a K. Mental health demands that we take our questions seriously and seek true answers. A tree that is nothing but an upright trunk is dead.

It still looks as if, at the bifurcation of the road, the majority will not track down all possible questions. Since Jefferson, America has been dreaming of universal public education, and we must not give up the dream. The facts, however, seem to support the pessimism of the Preacher: "All is vanity. . . . One generation passes away, and another comes, and the earth abides forever" (*Ecclesiastes* 1:2,4). And the generations all seem to move in the same old rut. For, said Heraclitus, "What wisdom, what understanding is theirs? They put their trust in bards and take the mob for their teacher, not knowing that the many are bad, and few good." (Diels, fragment 104. See Bakewell: *Source Book in Ancient Philosophy*, p. 34; Scribner's 1907.) But Heraclitus also said: "All human laws are fed by one divine law which has as much power as it wishes and is sufficient for all things and excels all things." (Diels, fr. 114. See Kirk and Raven 213, or Bakewell 34, or Milton C. Nahm, item 91.)

Plato, too, shared the ancient pessimism and, in his *Republic,* put the many under the rule of the few. For the latter he devises a rigorous lifelong system of education. Seeing that even the kings, like the many, will not become philosophers, Plato provides that the philosophically educated few will be drafted as rulers.

The American and the French Revolutions have brought forth the dream of general education, and the vicissitudes of our century make it likely that we must choose either to educate everybody capable of education, or to be ruled by dictators or, even worse, by the mob of Archie Bunkers, with the likelihood of an Atomic War.

And where does religion come into this picture? Precisely at the level of Archie who is cocksure that his is the right religion (which he practices as little as his vote), but who could (40) not give any intelligible account of what it is. Can you account of yours? Just where do you stand? And if, at the bifurcation, you have not turned to study, and therefore must depend on authorities, what is yours?

That brings us back to our immediate topic. What is the authority of ideas? I am now using the word idea in the Platonic (and Kantian and Hegelian) sense. The question seems far-fetched, but the answer is close at hand.

You do admit that some thoughts are true and some are not, though you may be uncertain which are which. Yet you admit that one really ought to try to find out. You also admit that you do not know everything. You may even see clearly that the phrase "to know everything" is fantastic as long as we do not know the future. Yet you will not respect any "no trespassing" sign anybody might try to erect in the domain of knowledge. You will not say that, since nobody knows now, the topic beyond our present reach is therefore unknowable. (What *is* unknowable, of course, is whatever amounts to a simple contradiction in terms, like a wooden nickel, or a square circle. And even that is known, as being a contradiction.) So you do admit that the search for knowledge cannot be stopped. And as you look at this "cannot" you find it is not compulsory like a feverish dream which goes on and on and drives you crazy because you cannot stop it. On the contrary, this "cannot," far from confining you, opens the way for your inquiry, and it is only your weariness which temporarily stops you. Tomorrow, when refreshed, you will continue the search. And if you die before you have found your answer, you know that another can pursue your question by making it his.

In short, you find that the very idea of truth has a hold on you, yet is not an obsession but instead the liberating experience of the freedom of reason.

I have just used the phrase "the *idea* of truth" and in so doing, I have used the word *idea* in a more specific sense than before. When Plato spoke of ideas he often meant what moderns would call concepts, such as the concept of a circle, or of an animal or a plant. But he also spoke of the idea of ideas. Let me illustrate. When you define the circle as the locus of all points equidistant from the center, this concept is valid of all circles, big or small. You might say the concept presides over everything that has circularity. Or when you roughly distinguish an animal from a plant by saying it can move from place to place, then this mobility is found in every animal. (To be sure, this is not a very good example since plants have their movements, too, and the coral animals cannot move from their place.) Everything circular comes under the concept of circle. But this concept in turn comes under conic sections, and these, algebraically, are quadratic equations, that is, a species of functions. Now Plato's question was, what is the idea which presides over all ideas? And he called it the idea of "the Good" (tò agathòn). If you ask him why he uses such a moralistic sounding word for his last word in logic, he tells you, in the *Phaedo,* 99c, that his Good also means obligation or "ought" (déon). All ideas *ought* to make sense, which means that inherently they do make sense and therefore make sense for anyone capable of grasping their meaning. To be sure, many of the ideas we humans have on our mind are not yet logically mature and merely should make sense; and if we want to take them seriously we know at least this much that, in the final analysis, they ought to be meaningful.

(41)   This then is the challenging idea of ideas. It is not spelled out, not definable. What is definable is always a specific idea which comes *under* the idea of ideas. The latter presides over all inquiry, and over all verity. It is not "cut and dried" as, to certain minds, some specific ideas seem to be. It is an inescapable and a live challenge. Using a phrase of Kant, you may call it the ground of possibility of all thought and all truth.

Plato has been called an idealist, and the name is not inappropriate if you mean by it that, for Plato, the idea of ideas is supreme. Once in a rare while he refers to it as "the god" (hò theós). But if by idealism you mean a theory, and by theory a doctrine which might be true yet also could turn out to be a mistake, you have missed Plato's point. Philosophers do not escogitate theories. They point out facts and verify them.

As a simple fact, we all stand under the idea of ideas. Things *ought* to make sense, and we ought to look for it. If this were not the case we could not think at all, that is, we could never even look for any meaning. True, our mind is an arguing activity, a ratiocinative mind; and if you look for the ground of possibility of ratiocination you will find it lies in the idea of truth. If truth were only a word, only human opinion, then all argumentation would be a meaningless mental motion without a real purpose.

(42)   It is the fact that the idea of truth has authority over us which makes us humans "rational animals." But never forget for a moment that this authority is not confining but liberating. The

(43) *Gospel of St. John* says (8:32) "the truth will make you free." (To be sure, this is said in a Christological context, which our Chapter VII will touch upon slightly. It is not a simple philosophical statement.)

So far I have endeavored to speak plain philosophy. However, this does not do away with the religious implications. Let us then cast a glance ahead and look at some statements by a very great theologian, one of the greatest though indirect followers of Plato, St. Augustine.

On page 4, I have already quoted his sentence that, "if

(44) there is nothing more excellent, then the truth itself is God."

Augustine asks where this truth is to be found. And in his

(45) comment *On Psalm 130* he warns you not to look for it in upper space, as if truth could be at any distance. "If those heights were to be searched, then the birds would beat us in the

(46) race toward God."

In his book *On True Religion*, Augustine wrote a few sentences which every student should know by heart. "Do not

(47) go outside; go back into yourself; in the inner man dwells truth; and if you find your human nature changeable, then go even deeper. But remember that when you transcend yourself you are transcending your ratiocinating soul. Therefore tend toward that whence the light of reason itself is lit. For where does every good ratiocinator arrive but at the truth? But the truth itself does not arrive at itself by ratiocination, for it is what the

ratiocinators seek. Behold there the coming together [of the seeking and its goal] higher than which there can be none; and join yourself to that togetherness. Confess that you are not it. For it does not seek itself. You however came to it seeking, so that the inner man could come together with his inhabitor, in the greatest and spiritual joy."*

For the moment let us hold fast two things. First that the idea of truth has authority over us. And second that this fact furnishes a key to theological statements which otherwise would seem an utterly unintelligible "speaking in tongues."

So much for the idea of truth.

Student Comments

Since students handed in only two direct questions regarding this chapter the following quotations from their term papers are good illustrations of their thinking with regard to passages in the text to which they refer indirectly.

For me, the fact that students complain about irreligious conditions in ecclesiastic custom is a sign of spiritual health. Some of our young people may succeed in replacing bad customs with better ones, fostering a deeper religiosity.

(37) "I think I should start with the school system and how it corrupts the young. Students in lower grades are usually scared to death to answer questions and speak out in class. They are afraid of what their classmates will say if their answer is wrong and the teacher reprimands them. The smaller children always ask honest questions honestly. They really want to know and

---

*de vera religione, xxxix,72. Noli foras ire; in te ipsum redi; in interiore homine habitat veritas; et si tuam naturam mutabilem inveneris, transcende et teipsum. Sed memento cum te transcendis, ratiocinantem animam te transcendere. Illuc ergo tende unde ipsum lumen rationis accenditur. Quo enim pervenit omnis bonus ratiocinator nisi ad veritatem? Cum ad se ipsum veritas non utique ratiocinando perveniat, sed quod ratiocinantes appetunt ipsa sit. Vide ibi convenientiam qua superior esse non possit; et ipse conveni cum ea. Confitere te non esse quod ipsa est: siquidem seipsam non quaerit: tu autem ad ipsam quaerendo venisti ... ut ipse interior homo cum suo inhabitore summa et spirituali voluptate conveniat.

are sincere in their approach. I believe this honesty and enthusiasm is lost with age and experience." Sophomore woman, Catholic, education major.

"My parents sent me to a Catholic grade school and high school. Here is where I was taught what to believe in. My religious experiences were forced on me. It did not bother me because I had no idea that I might want anything taught to me differently. The Church advises and I was the one to be advised. My experience was not of that personal form as was that of Bernadette at Lourdes. I believed because it was taught to me. My faith in my religion is now what is troubling me." Same student.

"When I was a child I faithfully attended church and knew all the stories, hymns, and accepted beliefs. I accepted God and the Kingdom of Heaven in the same way in which I accepted the fact that China and a race of Chinese people exist on the other side of the world. I continued to hold on to my image of God until I was in High School. During a lecture in a science course on the movement of electrons around a nucleus, I had my first religious experience. I began to wonder." Senior man, was Methodist, psychology major.

(38) "Even though I attended Catholic grade schools, I don't feel that I have a strong knowledge of Catholic doctrine. My training consisted of memorizing answers to catechism questions. Expressions of doubt were not encouraged. I became adept at stringing the right words together but it was simply drudgery and meaningless to me. I have now learned that there is not only nothing wrong in asking questions but it is my duty to do so." Junior woman, Catholic, English major.

"My thoughts and visions of what religion actually means were previously just pounded-in-stereotypes of something that I had to learn and accept in a Catholic grade school." Sophomore man, Catholic, no major.

(39) "Since I started school at the age of six, it seemed the best way to succeed in school was to do what the teacher said, don't ask

questions, memorize, and don't worry about why you are learning what you are. Well, maybe my teachers didn't mean it this way but that was the impression I got. I guess I came to this conclusion after what you said a student should be, a lover of knowledge and truth, and inquisitive. It made me feel bad because I have not lived up to my side of the bargain in my last four years while I attended college. . . . I never did like to make decisions and I guess the main reason is I never like to take responsibility. This is probably why I am in the shape I am in now, not knowing where to go or what to do, it always seemed easier to wander along and do what other people thought I should, without thinking about it myself. What really bothers me is I didn't care." Senior man, Catholic, mathematics major.

"But I don't think that, because one sets standards for himself, those standards are at all redemptive. If those standards lead to corruption and destruction, we might assume that revisions are in order." Junior woman, Baptist, education major.

"Accompanied with my doubts was the feeling inside of me that, just by having certain doubts, I was guilty of going astray, of somehow wandering away from the safety and saving power of what my religion held to be true. And out of an uneasy fear, I did not dare pronounce any of these doubts to those of my religious group. Strangely enough, though, I now do not feel any guilt or misgivings about the way I see some things." Senior woman, Baptist, Spanish major.

(40) "I have found out that there is more to religion than just going to church. In fact, going to church is probably the simplest part of religion. Being religious is something that is inside a person. The way a person shows his religion differs from anyone else's way of showing it." Senior man, Catholic, physical education major.

"Religion therefore should not be like a football game where rules have to be followed, but it should be a very special, and a very emotional experience in which the participant is wholly and completely involved, concerned, and aware of what his purpose is in regard to religion." Sophomore man, Catholic, no major.

"Religion does concern people who think; it is something which happens in the mind. For who can hear the voice inside of him if he does not think and listen to his own thoughts?" Sophomore woman, Catholic, education major.

(41)   "I haven't found the answers I was looking for. I am not even certain as to what the questions are, but there is something inside of me that demands to know more. Perhaps the answers are within me, and I must search myself (search my soul??) for the answers which I frequently and honestly ask myself—the questions I do know I ask." Junior woman, Lutheran, education major.

[My advice: Reading helps. The unfed soul will be caught in its own shrinking circle. The ecclesiastic talk about the supererogatory merits of the saints of which we can partake makes sense as soon as the hungry soul seeks nourishment with the seriousness you so well express.]

(42)   "If we believe just what people say, we will be no better off than a parrot that can only repeat what people teach him to say. He does not have a mind of his own to reason out what is right or wrong." Junior man, Catholic, physical education major.

(43)   "How can you succeed at Truth? You can only work toward it with all your being. For the seeker, there is no final Love, Truth, or Justice, but only the seeking. And there is no failure, providing we keep trying with all our being. Nor is there any competition. For if no one can think for me, if no one can assume my responsibility for me, then no one can compete with me toward my goal. Finally, each venture, each step, is a new beginning; each time we face a decision, weigh a doubt, or reflect on a problem, we must assert ourselves anew." Junior man, former Catholic, English major.

"In the different religions, we can see how God is revealing Himself to all men according to their personal capacities. ... Man can hardly be ultimately concerned about something he knows nothing about, and he definitely cannot be concerned about anything the moment he is brought into this world. Thus, it is very plain to see how religion is being destroyed in our world today. We are not allowing religion to grow and flourish, but we are making it a stale and unappealing object." Sophomore man, Catholic, no major.

(44) "If there is a challenge, need there be a challenger? If so, it may be the individual itself. Or perhaps even life itself. Indeed, the very existence of reality challenges us to find the truth of reality." Junior man, former Catholic, English major.

(45) "The scene of looking up in the heavens and worshipping God there, has led people to believe that God is a part time God, limited in his activity only to sacred places or sacred times. They imagine God as living only in a church and being awake only on Sundays." Sophomore man, Catholic, no major.

"It is a person's intelligence which causes him to question religious beliefs, but it also plays an important role. Intelligence helps a person to criticize and purify his ideas of what God is, and organize his life to give it significance. God reveals himself in different ways and a man grasps meanings that seem suitable to his way of thinking. . . . Symbols should not be mistaken for the Divine, because God is not an object." Sophomore woman, Methodist, psychology major.

(46) Q: "Using mythological language, you have said that the unconditionality of God makes essential claims upon the soul of man. But aren't 'claims' in the realm of the conditional?"

      A: Certainly, for we do live in that realm. And, indeed, the very Prophets wondered why God should want fallible men as his witnesses. And none of us is infallible when he says to himself, "*this* is what God wants." Tomorrow I may find I was mistaken. It is the *form* of the claim which is unconditional. I furnish the fallible content.

(47) Q: To what does St. Augustine refer when he says "the inner man"? Does he mean the "soul"?

A: Your question remains vague and unanswerable as long as you do not say what you mean by the word soul. The Greek word *psychè* indicates the presence of life in a thing, be it a plant or an animal. The very word animal derives from the Latin *anima* which the dictionary replaces by "soul." In this sense, whatever has a soul is animate. The inaminate is lifeless. If you believe in a life independent of the body, you can then ask where the soul is to be found once the body has died. However, that kind of question is mythological, that is, it takes for granted that body and soul are things, though the one is material, the other "spiritual." Both things have their proper whereabouts, and so the question would ask: *Where* is the spirit world? Or, as Descartes quite seriously asked, in which part of the brain is the soul located as long as the body is alive? The real question is whether terms like "where" and "location" apply at all to the non-mythological reality which can be designated by the word "soul." If that is the case, I should not say, "I have a soul," but rather, "I am a soul." In that sense, the soul is not an object at all, but a synonym for "I."

Nobody can look directly into your "inner man." In this respect, the mythological expression tells the plain truth when it says that God alone can see into the human heart. If by "soul" you mean "I," that is indeed what Augustine refers to. And if you keep that in mind while reading again the memorable passage, its every clause should become lucid.

Chapter V

THE CHALLENGE OF THE SUPERINDIVIDUAL, SUPERTEMPORAL IDEAS

"The norm grows within the medium of experience. But it is at the same time the criterion of any experience" (54). "Theonomy does not mean the acceptance of a divine law imposed on reason by a highest authority; it means autonomous reason united with its own depth" (85). "The claim of anything finite to be final in its own right is demonic" (134). (Paul Tillich: *Systematic Theology.* Volume I, University of Chicago Press 1951.)

"If the transcendence of the divine is asserted exclusively, religion declines into a slavish cultivation of superstitious practices and becomes pretty much what Sigmund Freud imagined it to be" (278). "The religious man would see the image of God in the individual person, whereas faith in culture is faith in universally binding supertemporal values which have exerted their effects in their respective historical spheres" (279). "The concept 'humanity' sums up that which gives to all human reality, to all human existence its tension, its orientation towards the supertemporal ideas of the true, the good, the just, and the beautiful" (238). "There is no way of enforcing the values which make life worth living directly; they attain reality only through freedom" (157). (Fritz Medicus: *On Being Human,* Frederick Ungar Publishing Co., New York 1973.)

(48)   The idea of truth is not the only form or manifestation of the *ought* under which we live and which makes us alive
(49)   mentally. No doubt, we ought to look for what is true. But we also ought to seek what is just, what is good, and what is beautiful.

(50)   Some philosophers have tried to define that to which the

words just, true, good, and beautiful point. They forget that
51)   these words do not designate fixed and therefore definable
entities, but instead are challenges. Definitions make sense only
within given objective contexts. A challenge, however, is an
appeal to a responsible subject. For instance, the idea of truth
challenges us to formulate objectively correct definitions, tenable
and unobjectionable within the appropriate universe of discourse, be it biology or jurisprudence, physics or philosophy.
Confronted by a specific problem, we have the task of discovering and determining just what is objectively so. Likewise if the
discourse is about justice, it is up to us to ascertain what is just;
for example, what is a fair tax, an equitable verdict, a viable
constitution. In each context we ought to seek what is just,
52)   true, good, and beautiful, and then clearly state it. Such
statements ought to be definite but they cannot be definitive.
53)   Tomorrow's problems demand amendments. Furthermore, different contexts yield different findings, all of them correct; in the
case of a statue we can find its weight, its price, its artistic
value, its psychological attractiveness or repulsiveness. It would
be a fantastic hope to collect "all possible statements." We do
not know the future. All we know is that we ought to stick to
our duty and not give up on account of weariness. Reality is a
going concern. There is no encyclopedic knowledge. Mythologi-
54)   cally speaking, "God alone knows it all." Our real hope is for
knowing properly whatever we do know, and doing right
55)   whatever we do, and stating clearly what we state.

Let us look at the challenge of the four ideas, one by one.
Justice is the basis. Hobbes spoke of a state of nature in which
man is a wolf to every other man—*homo homini lupus*—and
there is war of all against all. That waste of energy can be
prevented intelligently by the rule of law. Every social organization has its degree of efficiency. But to be efficient does not
necessarily mean to be equitable. The first book of Plato's
Republic makes it quite clear that the stronger or the smarter
one will efficiently use whatever happens to be the law, for his
own advantage. Sheer power cannot establish a just society. The
idea of justice tells us to give to each what is properly his. The
idea does not define what that is. It is we who, under the
challenge of the idea, ought to ascertain what is just, today for

today, and tomorrow for the new day. A society can thrive only if there is dependable justice. If injustice has corroded society and the state, insecurity makes life hard. Moreover it becomes difficult to heed the challenge of the true, the good, the beautiful. A corrupt state will try to boss not only political science and sociological theory but even such unpolitical disciplines as physics and biology. The conscientious search for truth is inhibited. And corruption need not have gone very far to ruin the writing of history; it is the victors who write it. Likewise, a corrupt society will replace artistic conscientiousness with the questionable taste of the majority, or of the clique in power. Corruption makes the state overbearing to the point where the authorities may try to lay down laws as to what is art and what isn't.

(56)   Justice furnishes the basis for a free society in which there is trust. And justice can be enforced. In a sound society it will be enforced. A Bill of Rights will be written, and the state will see to it that the laws are heeded. Unlike justice, goodness cannot be enforced, nor can one legislate about it. A sound state will make me pay not only my taxes but my private debts. But no state can justly force me to give alms. Of course, a totalitarian state will tell a citizen to "volunteer" or be penalized. And a bad school will try to penalize students for not "volunteering" work beyond the measure of what is required. A

(57)   quite different social organization, the church, in general recognizes that goodness cannot be enforced. If a church requires tithing, such contributions usually still retain the character of voluntary gifts. To be sure, exorbitant zeal may induce churchmen to legislate about all kinds of good actions. Maybe they do not realize that enforced goodness is no goodness at all, but sly selfishness; the would-be faithful come to believe they can gain salvation by services like contributions, or attendance, or self-castigation.

(58)   While the idea of the just rightly leads to legislation, the ideas of the good, true and beautiful are challenges addressed to the freedom of the human being. The saint, the scientist, the artist—none of them can do his true work except in freedom, that is, motivated by his personal interest and dedication. (I should not say the saint but simply the good man. All real saints

have stressed that they were still sinners. Ecclesiastic canonization comes after death.)

(59)   Chapter IV has already touched upon the necessarily free approach to truth. The very idea of the true forbids the kind of dogmatism which presents every truth as a dead fact merely to be memorized. Plato distinguished between opinion (dóxa), right opinion (orthé dóxa) and the clear demonstrable and demonstrated truth (epistéme) which alone liberates the mind. If without proof I merely believe in the theorem of Pythagoras and can recite that, in a right triangle, the sum of the squares over the legs is equal to the square over the hypothenuse, I have the right opinion but it makes me its slave who merely professes belief. Augustine said *credo ut intelligam*; I believe in order to understand. Only if I can prove to myself that the Pythagorean theorem is true does it free my mind (in the degree in which it is unquestionably true). Bad schools stop short of understanding and inculcate only right opinion. Corrupt schools do not even care whether an opinion is right, they indoctrinate their pupils with opinions which happen to be current. Sad to say, churches are not immune to the vices of schools. There are churchmen who have never heard of, or have not pondered Augustine's "I

(60)   believe so that I may understand." No wonder their authoritarianism ruins the trust of so many young people. Such churchmen will quote the letter and ignore the spirit of the Gospel of John who has his Christ say, "the truth shall make you free" (*John* 8:32). To be sure, John identifies the liberating truth with Christ himself, in whose mouth he puts the words: "I am the way and the truth" (*John* 14:6). And therefore, "the Son makes you free" (*John* 8:36). A magically minded reader would regiment us so that, like good soldiers, we would march the preordained way. But obedience is not yet love, though an unquestioning lover may simply obey. We, who cannot help asking questions, have asked whether responsibility can be imposed from without, and we have found it must be freely

(61)   taken. The host of the great supper merely invites his guests (*Luke* 14:16-17), he does not try to force them to come. Unlike stupid dictators, the Christ of the Gospels does not believe in the efficacy of force (*Matthew* 26:52). As for the truth, how can it set you free, if you are afraid to ask (*Luke* 9:45)? The

(62)   truth requires honest study. Poor churchmen like poor teachers
would reduce study to regimentation.

Like the good and the true, the beautiful requires freedom.
In fact, the liberating function of beauty is basic in education.
The little child who comes running to mother to show her the
beautiful flower he found, or who has discovered the beauty of
a simple melody, even the appeal of a silly ditty, has discovered
the fact that he finds himself a free appreciator (though of
course he is quite incapable as yet to speak about himself in
such academic words). His excitement shows the liberation that
has taken place in him. Schiller wrote a famous essay *On the
Aesthetic Education of Man* (1793/94) and, a century before,
Shaftesbury's *Inquiry Concerning Virtue* (1699) spoke of "the
common and natural sense of a sublime and beautiful in things."
Our contemporary, Hans Urs von Balthaser, has written a
magnificent "theological aesthetic" with the title *Herrlichkeit*
(Johannes Verlag, Einsiedeln 1961-69) which would rest theology on the divine *Glory*. The last fifty years, our American
schools have swung around from considering art as "frills" to a
more or less serious cultivation of taste. People who know will
agree that the affliction of our underprivileged seems to be
aesthetic more than economic poverty. This is quite obvious in
the realm of language. Obviously, we have hardly begun the
remedy which is to help children and adolescents to the freedom
of clear and personal speech. But we do live in a period of
renascence. All you have to do is to compare today's fashion
magazines with the styles of 1900.

Now to the main point of our chapter. The four ideas or
values—the just, the true, the good, the beautiful—are not
independent, like autonomous parts. They are four different
aspects or manifestations of one and the same reality. As a
student interested in philosophy you will judge these pages with
regard to the truth they try to present. But you cannot so judge
them without, at the same time, evaluating the language and
finding it either clear or muddled. Nor can you ignore the moral
purpose, that is, the educational intention of this writing. And
you cannot abstract from the question whether it is just for me,
the writer, to address you, in your dignity of a believer or an

unbeliever, in words like mine which, in your ears, may sound mawkishly sanctimonious or else like rank infidelity. These four values are four aspects of one and the same writing, and what goes for this writing is also true with regard to any cultural document and any human action.

The question then is: What does all this have to do with our study of religion?

The title of our chapter calls the four ideas superindividual and supertemporal. The first adjective seems plain. When any one of us calls anything just, or true, or good, or beautiful, he does not express a mere individual preference. When I say, "This is unjust," I do not mean it is to my disadvantage. An unjust ruling can benefit me financially, but my individual gain does not make it just. When I call a statement true, I mean it will stand up under investigation. In contrast, I know that a sly lie will not, although my presenting a falsehood as if it were a truth may induce my listener to abstain from any investigation. When I call an action good, I do not merely point out that it is good for some individual or some group nor even for mankind. Likewise, the beautiful is not merely what happens to (63) be in line with current taste, although beauty does require taste (64) for being appreciated. The four words, just, true, good, beautiful (65) express validities, not preferences. In fact, we often emphasize (66) our words by saying, for instance, this is "*truly* beautiful" or that is "not good *at all*." We do of course express our own view, but our concern is not so much with our individual reaction as with reality itself.

As for the supertemporal nature of the ideas, it may have become clear to the meticulous reader that the four ideas are not four yardsticks but a fourfold invitation to judge for ourselves. Nobody can define what is beautiful or good, or true at that, once and for all. Definitions are intellectual endeavors, and as time passes, we find we have to redefine and define better what we may have mistaken for a final formula. The challenge pervades time and thus proves its authority over any temporal formulation or action.

I have repeatedly used the word "challenge." And you may (67) have asked: Who is the challenger? If I may use a good old word, I answer simply: God! But you are right, of course, in reminding me that that is a mythological term and, as such, can easily mislead a reader who has the habit of meaning by God a personage in the sky or, if he is more sophisticated, "a supreme power." The trouble is not so much with mythological terminology as with a literal interpretation thereof, as Chapter II pointed out. If God were a celestial potentate his every word addressed to man would be an order rather than a challenge. Now, an order can be ignored, the way we all ignore the 45 mile speed limit suggested by the signs at the entrance of our campus. Of course we may get a ticket, but we are taking that chance. In contrast, when I speak of the challenge of the four ideas, I mean to point at something that has an inexorable hold on us,

(68) whether we heed it or try to ignore it. And insofar as the word God can designate the very ground of all reality (in popular parlance, designate the Creator) without which nothing that is could be, I dare say that the fourfold challenge is simply the Will of God with regard to man. And no matter how we twist and turn, we cannot get out from under it.

How do I prove that? I do not, except by inspecting the matter in my own self. And there I find it is so, the four ideas have a hold on me; in fact, they alone make it possible for me to experience myself as a self. (In that respect the word Creator is not bad.) As for you, all I can say is go ahead and find out

(69) for yourself. What is the ground of your freedom?

A few years ago, one of our philosophy majors said: Let us *do* philosophy, instead of talking about it. Go ahead and do it.

Student Questions

(48) Q: Are we seeking the challenge individually or as a human race?

A: It is not an "either/or." The race is not a self and therefore is under no challenge. This fact makes it possible for individuals to say that, merely as members of the species, they have no obligations and can follow their whims. To be sure, like any other animal, man will often find that the will of others or the conditions of surrounding nature furnish obstacles to the pursuit of his whims. However, the race is human because the individual selves can acknowledge the existence of the challenge and try to live up to it. Almost all individuals can do that, once they are out of earliest infancey. And the relatively few cases of severe natural limitation, e.g., of mongoloid retardation, still leave the rest of us with the challenge to treat even them as human.

(49) Q: Does everyone seek the inner meaning of *all* the challenges? It seems that many people lack the "beauty of words" yet still make an attempt to find it.

A: Quite so. We all have our natural limitations, and they may be serious under the given circumstances. For instance, in university study precision of speech is indispensable. It may lack artistic beauty, but as simple prose it must be clear.

(50) Q: If the four challenging ideas are unconditional, how can each individual determine what is good, just, true, and beautiful, if not by conditional means?

A: You are right, it is precisely the human situation to live in a conditional world, and the conditions include our own talents or the lack thereof. Therefore we had better keep at the lifelong work of coming to know ourselves, as the only way we have of determining, under the given circumstances, just what is the specific meaning of each one of the four ideas and of their joint challenge.

(51) Q: According to Tillich, "religious is what concerns me unconditionally." Is this like saying, forget reality and exist on ideals alone?

A: On the contrary, such frightful forgetting would make us the victims of every changing mood welling up in our individuality. We would not be *out* of reality but trapped *in* its most limited form, caught in our own skin, as it were. And for a person thus imprisoned in his

individuality there arises indeed the question to be or not
to be. Suicidal tendencies show that our being caught in
such a trap cannot amount to unconditional concern. That
is why the objectivistic talk of the religions can remind us
that "this life" is not all, and that "the next life" matters
more. Such talk, of course, turns ideas into fixed things,
like set rules which then, the same kind of talk must call
"revealed from beyond." The latter designation acknowl-
edges that the ideas are "beyond" the conditional.

(52) Q: Would the negatives of the challenges, that is, what is
not just, good, true and beautiful, also be challenges? And
could we arrive at the state of justice, goodness, truth and
beauty by seeking the "truths" of their negatives?

    A: The mythological answer to your first question is:
Yes, the challenges of the Devil! And, as you know from
the *Book of Job,* or from the Prologue in Heaven of
Goethe's *Faust,* God uses the Devil for his own purposes.
Or, in another mythological expression, the Devil is only a
fallen angel. He has no power of his own. Like the power
of the gods, the power of the devils is borrowed from, and
is a perversion of the authority of God.—Mind you, I am
not denying the very real existence of such powers. Who
among us has never been tempted to lie, or to return
injustice for injustice? Who has never been careless in his
choice of words? Who has never felt like the fool who says
in his heart, there is no God? (*Psalms* 14:1 and 53:1) The
Vulgate calls this fool *insipiens,* that is, one who is not
sapiens, who simply does not know and therefore speaks
and acts unwisely. In our time, such ignorance is being
inculcated in us, from childhood on, instead of being
replaced by deeper insight. (A case of such better insight is
the topic of our next chapter.)—As for your second question, an affirmative answer is likewise possible. If we find
the truth of the negation, we may arrive at the true idea.
For instance, *Psalm* 10:4 seems to explain that it is the
exasperation of being entrapped in one's sin which prevents
"the fool" from even asking the question what the word

"God" could truly mean. He blindly assumes it must mean a world dictator. And seeing that no such dictator's revenge has yet retaliated for his sins, he says there is no God. The truth of this negative statement is that "there is no such dictator god." In some such manner you can arrive at truth by the negative route. But of course you must not draw the false inference like the boy in Sunday school who, being asked what is the first step toward forgiveness of sin, answered: "Why, to sin!" You do not have to drive into every dead end street of town to reach your destination; it is more sensible to ask for the right way. To be sure, there are times when, in matters of religion, you may not readily receive the right answer.

(53) Q: Each of the challenges of life,—truth, goodness, beauty and justice,—will differ in interpretation from individual to individual. Therefore how can there be an efficient form of government, or a united world?

A: By discussion! The Roman principle of justice was, *audiatur et altera pars,* listen to what the other fellow has to say! In other words, give up the notion of any final solution. The Nazi "final solution" for the trumped up Jewish question was Auschwitz, and some American hawks advocated bombing the Vietnamese out of existence. If people have the good will to find an equitable settlement, and if they are sufficiently educated, they can always find an equitable settlement which will work till the next amendment comes due.

(54) Q: Since for every man there is a way that seems right to him, how is mankind to know the Real Truth (God, the Will of God)?

A: The real truth is that there is no final formulation. It is the Will of God that we evaluate each new problem on its own merits, giving each its due. This is in line with Aristotle's basic principle of justice: To each what is his! If there were a final formula it would mean the death of all life. However, if conscientiously and sensibly worded, a formula can be a crutch and an energy saver. The bad side of every formula is that temporarily it can save us from conscience, can apparently shield us from "the eye of God."

(55) Q: Do you believe everyone has a conscience? Does conscience stem from what you were taught as a child?

      A: Conscience is what you *do* conscientiously, not what you *have*, like a skull. Aristotle has long pointed out that virtue is acquired by habit. Make it a habit to speak clearly and you will become a good speaker. For instance, what do you mean by being "taught as a child"? What should it mean "to teach"? To indoctrinate or rather to encourage inquiry? Deadening dogma and unquestioning belief? Or else up-to-date definitions (which is what Ecumenic Councils claim to write) and, as a result, a confident faith? I would not call conscience the fearsome knuckling under of those whose very bodily stance shows that they seem to expect a blow on the head. Real conscientiousness is the courage to have a critical look at oneself and eventually at the historical circumstances; to distinguish between the better and the not-so-good course, and to prefer the former. And that is not so-called pride but rather the humility of knowing that none of us is infallible. In this respect, everyone *ought* to develop a conscience. And we ought to help others who, as yet, are slaves of indoctrination.

      Comment of a fellow student: "The conscience cannot always distinguish between good and bad. This is what makes a person human and adds knowledge to life."

(56) Q: Why are people so prone to join groups? If the "I" and the four challenges addressed to the "I" are so much more important to the person than the "me," why don't more people choose a life of seclusion and personal happiness rather than one of conformity and dogmatism?

A: The challenge of truth sends me to the seclusion of the study, the library, the laboratory; the challenge of beauty requires the seclusion of the studio; and the challenge of goodness objects to publicity (*Matthew* 6:3 "When thou givest alms, do not let thy left hand know what thy right hand is doing.") But the challenge of justice makes me come out into the public. It demands group action so that justice can be enforced. What monarch is so fair that whatever he decides to enforce is just? We do our *thinking* on justice in seclusion. But our decisions are likely to be just only in the open forum.

You are right, of course, when you point out that the public is not necessarily just. If addicted to conformity and dogmatism, the group's decision will be unjust in all likelihood. No group as such is a responsible "I." Responsibility must be taken by the individual. And justice demands, as already pointed out in (53) above, that we listen to different opinions, and never claim that our decisions are unquestionably just. An unjust group can unanimously vote for a law that is patently unjust. And that causes the mental discomfort which makes us long for the happiness of seclusion.

(57) Q: Why have all the cultures since man's appearance in the world been based on a "religion"?

A: Man depends on the unconditional. He wants the peace of certainty. To be sure, art affords such peace. Schopenhauer said a work of art is like a quiet harbor into which we can flee from the storms and billows of the open sea. Yet we can not stay there forever, as the addicts to television and radio seem to hope; even genuine music stops at the end of the piece. Like beauty, truth also affords peace which comes with the cogency of our insights. Yet each insight simultaneously brings along new questions. And it is rather obvious that goodness and justice are very conditional. Furthermore, although the four challenges are not utterly separated, they still point in different directions, and none of them, as such, address the whole man.

For instance a good scholar is not necessarily a just man, and the widespread notion that artists are not "good people" is not entirely unmotivated. The religious challenge however concerns me unconditionally. Now, to be sure, a mind which lacks the discipline demanded by the idea of truth, easily misinterprets the unconditional challenge of religion as a dictatorial marching order. In fact, from his very beginnings, man was inclined to fancy the gods as dictators easily offended by disobedient subjects. And this is why religion can not be pure and sound without reason guided by the idea of truth.

(58) Q: Do you feel that our world is too organized, too dull, and thus causes all the young movements?

      A: Do you mean to say that the idea of justice, though basic for sound social life, can lead to organization for organization's sake? Yes, justice cannot exist if truth, beauty and goodness are ignored. Plato said of the sheer organization men, the watchdogs of his *Republic,* they cannot furnish a just state. In the twenties, partly as a result of the First World War, our young rebels protested against the rather rigid organization of the churches, and the dead memory work in schools. George Counts suggested the school might yet build a new social order. It did not. I for one have the impression that the present stirrings among young people go deeper. In fact I hope they will go beyond mere protest. As far as they have an outspoken religious appeal, they seem to be in danger of either relapsing into rigid regimentation or else petering out in sheer emotionalism. It is my hope that students as students will do their part, which is personally motivated study, especially of cultural history, particularly of our occident.

(59) Q: If the finding of truth is the goal of religion, and if the different religious leaders understand this and also realize that this goal is reached in as many ways as there are people, then why are they constantly trying to sell their product as the only way to truth?

A: In our present civilization not many religious leaders seem to understand what you point out. This is due partly to the absence of philosophical instruction, but mostly to a simple psychological fact which outsiders are prone to overlook. What you call the product of religious leaders is not really of their own making; although they often rearrange their "revelations," that is, those overpowering visions or verbal formulations, the revealing imagery has come upon them (as they say, "from heaven"). And since, to them, it has come as a gift, they feel they ought to share it with others. Furthermore, to them, these "revelations" constitute religion; their own religion, of course, but that is all the religion they know and, therefore, so they conclude, the only religion, and everybody's whom they can convert.

If you have ever fallen in love, why, instead of courting your beloved, should you go and play the field? And, psychologically, "getting religion" is very much like falling in love. Still another comparison: Most Americans speak only English; since, for them, English *is* language, why should they learn another? Or, again: If you are content in your own home and family, why upset yourself and yours by shopping around for possible alternatives?

(60) Q: Do you feel Augustine's writings were a product of the historical situation of turmoil, or could Augustine see through the situation, and is this the reason for his writing's endurance through the ages?

A: Sometimes I wonder who has taught American students always to put their questions as alternatives, in a harsh "either/or." As your own clause, "see through the situation," clearly shows, the answer is yes to both halves of what you say. How can you even imagine a man outside of his own historical situation? Robinson Crusoe survives, not nowhere but on his island, and when his man Friday shows up, he takes him into the situation. And among ourselves, even Trappist monks, pledged to silence, and cloistered from the world, are still part of our world, in which, for instance, they sell their produce, cheese and honey, and into which each one of them was born in the first place. As for Augustine, I believe as you do. His greatness is due. to his understanding of the historical situation. True, he understood it his own way. While contemporary defenders of the old Roman religion argued that the Visigoth sack of Rome, 410 A.D., was due to the neglect of sacrifice to the gods, Augustine argued that, on the contrary, it was the way the Christian God reminded them that they should give up those false gods. I am picking on this partisan side of Augustine's book, *The City of God.* There are many passages in that book and especially in many profounder books by him, which present a deeper insight, some of whose formulations I have already quoted in these pages. Along with Plotinus who influenced him, though perhaps only indirectly, Augustine is the one among the ancients who most emphatically was impressed by the superdenominational God who "teaches us from our innermost." This is why during our enterprise here, I am fond of quoting Augustine. He is keenly aware of the "challenge" (as I have called it for short, and in order not to shock my students; the fundamentalists would be shocked by the boldness of Augustine's formulations, and the self-styled atheists would be shocked even by the phrase "Will of God.")

(61)   Q: If one should fail when "challenged," would his conscience bother him as it does in a Catholic when his conscience is fully developed?

A: Yes, indeed. However I cannot keep from remarking on the quaintness of your formulation. Do Catholic consciences differ from others, in being fully developed (like the body of a youth who has attained his full height)? Or does not the word conscience indicate that the unending inner watchfulness is always open to new challenges? Of course, I understand what you mean. As St. Paul pointed out, the very young must be fed on milk. Later, when we become fit to be on our own, you can say our conscience has matured; though who can boast his is "fully" mature?

(62) Q: Since it is necessary for the church to appeal to the older people because they have the means and the will to support it, rather than to the young who seek change and would prefer turning from money to the practice of what is preached, what then can be done in organized religion to make that change?

A: Take vows of poverty. The artist and the student do it. The Catholic church expects it of its priests. Poverty is no particular blessing nor is it a virtue. But it is a great means of liberation as St. Francis saw. It sets us free do so what we *ought* to do, rather than cater to the current whims of "the world." There is also another thing I would say, taking my cue from the priest's phrase in the introit of the Mass, *sum indignus,* I am unworthy to come to the altar. Since the priest reads Mass not for himself alone but for all the faithful, are not all unworthy? Maybe every church worship should start with a prayer, "Dear Lord, forgive us for being a church!" For, the temptation of every organization is to take itself for an end rather than a means. And the temptation of churches, as already implied in the three preceding answers, is to consider themselves and not God alone as the only way to salvation, in fact, even to consider themselves as the certified purveyors of salvation. Of course this would be a hard lesson to accept in many a congregation. As for poverty, in some "low down" churches out in the sticks, preaching carries no remuneration. And some churches, like the Mormon, use their money chiefly for the needy. However, unpaid preachers may also lack all the scholarship which nowadays is so necessary. This is one argument in favor of state churches, like those of the Swiss cantons. If the state pays the preacher and therefore has the right to demand of him university studies to approximately a doctoral level, and if it also pays for the upkeep of the buildings, then the congregation is free to decide on real charity projects, and the preacher is set free from fixing his eye on the collection plate. But back to your question. What you can do in your church, if you belong to one, is to set up free instruction. A whiff of fresh university air would do nobody any harm. And you must, of course, not try to force your oldsters to indulge in such breathing exercises.

(63) Q: Do the words truth, beauty, justice and goodness convey the same meaning today as they did, let us say, in 475 B.C.? Since man has changed throughout time wouldn't the meanings the words imply necessarily have changed as well? Therefore truth, beauty, goodness, justice are general terms.

A: If you will, they are not "terms" at all, that is, they "terminate" nothing but, on the contrary, they always open up our own responsibility. This is why I have called them "ideas," in the sense of "challenges." Now if, like myself, you have no objection to the phrase "Will of God," then that phrase can be taken either mythologically, or else philosophically. Some mythologies turn the Will of God into a set of unchanging rules, which then often require the wildest contortions of the interpreter in order to make them at least halfway applicable to the changed conditions. On the other hand, the philosophical stress is precisely on the challenge (which you schoolishly call "general terms"), and then this Will of God is indeed directed at all times, being addressed to responsible beings who freely take their responsibility. Responsibility cannot be imposed. Then everything comes alive, and you can even speak of a "living God."

(64) Q: Are truth, justice, goodness and beauty more adherently sought by Christians and other believers, than by others? It seems to me that a believer in God would be more likely to search for these ideas and their meaning, and the attainment of this goal would serve as a reward, and would replace the reward-and-punishment morality and the merely negative enforcement notion of Hell.

A: I heartily agree with you that the mercenary pursuit
of rewards and the cringing fear of punishment are worldly
self-seeking ways and not true morality which seeks good
simply because it is good. What I have just said has long
been pointed out, even by atheists. I should even say that a
true morality comes with a true piety. Piety says it is a
privilege to "serve God." Why should I be rewarded on top
of it? Now, as for your question, who would deny that
there are both, pious Christians (I should say they are the
real ones) and also self-seeking reward-hungry make-believe
Christians? Theism is no criterion, and atheism is no
barrier. Buddhism is a very selfless atheistic religion. To say
it with *Matthew* 7:16 "By their fruits you will know
them."

(65) Q: How does man come to see the eternal ideas? Since it
seems that this realm can not be reached by going through
the objects of sense, how does man come to know?
Augustine claims our minds are illumined by God himself,
but how does this come about?

A: Oh, but they are reached very precisely "by going
through the objects of sense" and by not letting the objects
serve as obstacles and excuses. How does one see goodness?
Not by the excuse of priest and levite who argue legally
that the blood of the man left on the wayside by the
robbers would defile their clean garments; not by regarding
the bleeding wretch as an object, and as an obstacle to
their temple service; but by seeing through the mere
objectivity and thus finding one's duty to help, as the
Samaritan finds it. (*Luke* 10:30-35) How, in your own
present case, do you find the meaning of the idea of truth,
when you are puzzled by the expression "illumined by
God." That phrase may sound like the description of an
eye doctor who, with his mirror, illumines the inside of
your eye, or a radiologist who shoots his x-rays clear
through your body and comes up with a photograph of
your bones. In these cases, you are entirely passive, a mere
object to be investigated by the doctor. But Augustine has

warned you not to go outside when you seek God but to go back into the "inner man" where truth dwells. Of course, "inner" is a space word which obviously does not mean your liver or your brain. So what do you actually do? You do see that such objectivistic ways of talking get you nowhere. You take your intellectual responsibility and ask the question "how does this come about?" It comes about precisely by your initiative. All you have to do is to reflect and say: "Behold, I have just acted as a true I. It is I who have asked and been serious." And unless the word truth had its meaning (you cannot call your guesses or your bewilderment true), unless you found yourself challenged by the search for truth (you seek it, you have not created it) you could not even ask your question. So, if you have no squeamish objection to the word God, you must confess that God has just illumined you by means of that bewildering phrase, and by means of Augustine's help, and even of my words.

(66) Q: I think you are letting a lot of people off the hook by *only* demanding of them that they do their best to strive for justice, goodness, truth and beauty. For, do not all people do their best, considering their conditions? It does not seem to be a very evolutionary moral code.

       A: It is not the task of philosophy to write codes. In order to do that you must be sure you have a direct line to heaven! You are right of course that we all always have the handy excuse that we did our best, especially considering the conditions. We all also know what a foul excuse it is. Our philosophical purpose is to inquire into the truth of religious language which, indeed, is sometimes weird. And I still submit that the truth with regard to the four ideas is that they are challenges which we cannot dodge no matter how we squirm. They are precisely *not* spelled out codes. If they were we could always excuse ourselves by saying we did not know the language or that we misunderstood it. And in that way many an ecclesiastic prescription lets you off the hook, by really saying: Simply do as you are told and, by means of such "soldiering" throw the responsibility on the Big Boss.

(67) Q: Could not the feeling of guilt, and the belief in right and wrong, have its basis in the Godhead, and not come totally from society's conditioning?

A: Most certainly. Society can condition us, and we can either conform or renege. But we students know very well that real questions stick in us like harpoons. If we want to find tenable answers to our questions we must face them boldly. And in order to do so we must do our home work, that is, our reading up on the matter at hand. Some medievals called God the Hound of Heaven, and indeed, like a bulldog he will not let us off. But this is no bite that hurts unless we try to dodge it. It is the way to liberation which, for the student, comes with possible answers to serious questions. Of course, in order to let them be serious we must learn to formulate them adequately.

(68) Q: Cannot the word "God" be misleading? Someone sarcastically called God a gaseous vertebrate in the sky. Lots of people imagine that God is "up there"; is that not a mistake?

A: Indeed it is. Augustine said that if God were "up there" the birds would beat us to him. (Commentary on *Psalm* 130) As for the word, I once asked my teacher, Medicus, why he used the word. He replied: "There is none better." The trouble is its gender. Jews, Christians and Moslems speak of "Him," but Ramakrishna (1836-1886) of "Her," the Great Mother, whose priest he was.

(69) Q: Do you mean that whatever I feel is true is truly true?

A: By no means. There is logical cogency, and it can be quite impersonal as in a mathematical proof. But here we are concerned with a deeper certainty, a personal commitment which Fichte would call act, not fact. See Chapter II, (28).

Chapter VI

THE OSTENSIBLE PROOFS FOR THE SO-CALLED EXISTENCE OF GOD

> *"Proof as furnished by the intellect demonstrates how one item depends on another. If the existence of God is to be proven in this manner, it means that the being of God is supposed to depend on something else. Thus one can see at once that something wrong must result since God, as the very ground of everything, cannot be dependent on anything else."* Hegel: *Logik* (VI,76).

> *"Cause and substance are categories of finitude. The 'first cause' as "a being which initiates the causal chain would itself be a part of the causal chain and would again raise the question of cause" (209). "The connotation of something or someone who might or might not exist is the way in which the idea of God is understood today in scholarly as well as in popular discussions about the 'existence of God.' God does not exist. He is being-itself beyond essence and existence. Therefore, to argue that God exists is to deny him" (205).* Paul Tillich: *Systematic Theology.* Volume I (University of Chicago Press 1951).

◆ ◆ ◆

The meaning of certain terms is strictly relative. Used absolutely, they are meaningless. Galilei pointed out that the phrase "absolute motion" makes no sense. When we say a thing moves slowly or fast, we tacitly assume that our hearer knows what other thing we have in mind relatively to which our "moving" thing moves. A car moves relatively to the road. If it goes at what we call fifty miles per hour, and if it passes another car going at the same speed in the opposite direction, then the speed of each relative to the other is a hundred miles per hour. — The Americas have been moving slowly away from

88

the old continents. A space rocket moves away from the earth and towards Mars. And if you tell a fidgety child riding in your car to stop moving, you do not mean for him to get out and stand still by the roadside, but to stop moving relative to the car.—In order to measure velocity or acceleration, you need a frame of reference; for instance you count the evenly spaced telephone poles on the roadside. They do not move relative to the road, but they keep moving with the earth, relatively to the sun and the moon.

Now, existence is a term with relative meaning. Hamlet exists in Shakespeare's play but not in the history of Denmark. Jack's beanstalk exists in the fairy tale but not in the world of botany. The letters you see exist on this sheet of paper, but the meaning of the words exists in your mind and not on any paper.

It is obvious that there are many kinds of existence, physical and psychological, literary and historical, imaginable and conceptual. In ordinary talk, we do not bother to point out which kind we mean. If we wanted to speak very pedantically we should have to add a qualifying word or phrase stating what kind of existence. Sometimes we do just that. We say, "this is just your imagination." Or we ask, "did you really see it with your own eyes."

To prove the existence of anything means to demonstrate that it can be found in a certain universe of discourse, or in several. Among the chemical elements you can find oxygen but not phlogiston. However phlogiston exists in eighteenth century chemical theory. The incandescent electric bulb existed in the mind of Edison as an engineering possibility, but not yet in physical reality before he had made a workable specimen. Your first million exists in your wishful thinking and maybe even in your economic capability but not yet in your bank.

It is odd that most people, when speaking of existence,
(70) think only of two kinds of existence, material and magical. Of
(71) course, many will not readily admit that they believe in magic. They prefer to sweep their magical desires under a verbal rug; instead of magical they say spiritual. Others are squeamish about being called materialists. Such patterns of thinking and feeling are characteristic of the civilization in which a man lives.

There used to be a prankster trick of laying a wallet on the sidewalk with a string attached to it, and of pulling it away when a person reached for it. This is a good enough description of the prank you play on yourself more than on others when you speak of the existence of God without qualifying what kind of existence you mean. You toss out what looks like a profound problem, and you snatch it away, not with a string but with the trick of not saying what kind of existence you have in mind. It is likely that you have none at all but merely the vague word existence. Your trick is mentally invisible to your self, just as the prankster's string is physically invisible to the one who stoops for the wallet.

(72)
(73)   Now then, what kind of existence could be attributed to God? What do you mean by the word God? In our civilization it is probable that you mean what people vaguely call the Creator of the universe. It is also likely that you are convinced that the universe exists in all its kinds of existence, physical and mental. Since the creator comes first (though not necessarily in time) and the creation follows, then, if the universe exists so does its Creator. This is one of the favorite proofs for the "existence" of God. Of course it is not conclusive. Your opponent will hold that the universe is everlasting in its very nature and therefore does not need a creator.

(74)   You may want to advance a more sophisticated "proof," arguing with our Chapter V, that the supertemporal ideas are what is for us the real Will of God. And since we cannot deny the challenging existence of the just, the true, the good, and the beautiful, as challenges, the challenger is what the word God could and should mean. This is all very well as long as you admit the challenge as challenging you. But what about the infidel who, taking mythology literally, sees in God a personage, a conditional entity which he is willing to defy? For him your "proof" simply begs the question. Furthermore, having now a God of justice, truth, goodness and beauty, what can you say about nature? How did it come into existence? Or is it everlasting? Or how does our Challenger "create" nature? What do you mean by the verb, to create? Are you begging the question again?

(75)
(76)   "Is there a God?" you ask. How can anyone even try to answer you as long as you do not say what you mean by the

(77) word God? You say, something bigger than man; but so is an ox, so is the sun. You say, more powerful, but so is an elephant or an atomic bomb. You say, a spiritual being; but so is the Devil; and so is your soul, at that. So you turn on me and, referring to the previous chapters, you say God is the being with inescapable authority. But Buddha will tell you that authority is not a person.

(78) Are there any gods at all? Why, yes, all the gods men have ever believed in and served. Some still hold their authority like Allah, Brahma, even the deified Buddha of superstitious Buddhists. Others exist only in past history, or as poetic and dramatic figures. But you do not mean, "is there a god"; you ask, "is God?" What is God?

(79) The real question, then, is not about the existence of a god (or goddess), like the existence of Zeus or Aphrodite in the mind of the ancient Greeks, or the existence of Tezcatlipoca in the belief of the Aztecs who annually sacrificed to the god the youth who, during the year, had been treated as if he were the god himself. The character and service of all the gods men have ever worshipped is the topic of historical study. Our real question is about the essence of the God who is "behind" all the gods who are but masks of the divine. Sometimes these masks look more devilish than divine. But all the gods, as long as they have any faithful followers, do claim inescapable authority. And in order to do so, they have had to claim also the power over nature.

(80) As historical figures the gods can be studied. Our intellect can ascertain their always relative power and the culturally conditioned form of their authority. Likewise, their existence is relative; triumphantly they invade and subjugate human minds, and they rule over centuries, even millennia; and then they exist only in historical memory although, at times, they make a re-entry into historical existence. Carl Gustav Jung pointed out that, in many ways, the Nazi religion in Germany under Hitler, was a return to Wotan.

(81) It is also an historical problem, to ascertain the degree to which every religion presents only a mask of the divine; and, in that respect, the Kingdom of God is still veiled, and men wait for its arrival in full glory at some future time.

But all this does not do away with the real question, which appears to be the question regarding the essence of God. For the intellect cannot but distinguish between essence and existence. In the case of the gods, the distinction holds. Even if, losing all their believers, they lose their existence, they retain their essence in the findings of the historian.

The distinction does not apply to God. Thomas Aquinas raises the question "whether in God essence and existence are the same"—*utrum in Deo sit idem essentia et esse*—and he answers affirmatively, "that God *is* not only his essence but also his existence." He refers to Hilary of Poitiers who said that "existence is not an accident in God," that is, it is not accidental or merely for a time, as it is in the gods. (*Summa Theologica*, Part I, Q.3, Art.4.)

Proofs pertain to what the Scholastics call an accident and what we would be inclined to call a quality. When the chemist has synthesized a new compound, the medical man will ask whether it has any healing quality. If it proves to be a cure for some specific affliction, it will cure only by being applied, by the "accident" of being applied, and not by its mere essence. Similarly, the gods become efficacious "by accident," that is, when their image strikes receptive minds. But in God there is no accident, nothing that either occurs or does not occur, is manifest or is merely possible. Aristotle's God was pure act. The Scholastics agree; there is no passive potency in God.

(82)
(83)

The essence of the gods is within reach of the historian, and the psychologist can study their potency. But their potential effects occur only under given circumstances. Wotan could make his return only under the psychotic conditions prevailing in Hitler Germany. But the presence and actuality of God does not depend on favorable circumstances. If the minds of men are not receptive then, to put it in the language of the religions, God is present as God's Wrath.

To be sure, the historian has the duty to prove this form of presence by documents, which he must be able to read in their real historical meaning. (In our secularized civilization, such an appropriate reading cannot always be taken for granted. Nor are our schools very efficient in teaching any such realistic reading.) The right reading does not turn the "existence" of God into an "accident" of his "essence," an "accident" whose presence could be established only by a proof.

Schelling said, "there is no proof of the existence of God as such, because there is no existence of God as such. God's existence is immediately specific." (XI,571) [Written in his last years, possibly as late as 1854. See XI, v, ff.]

Of course Schelling is not talking about a God whose essence implies merely a potential existence, a God about whom one could ask the question: "Is there a God?" That question treats God as an object which might be but also might not be.
(84)   Objects are conditional entities. Their reality depends on the conditions. And that requires proof.

In his *Letters on Dogmatism and Criticism* of 1795, Schelling, at twenty, had written: "As soon as we enter the domain of proofs, we enter the territory of what is conditional." (I,308) In his *Aphorism* 52 of 1805/06, Schelling wrote (VII,150): "In no kind of knowledge can God occur as *known*, as object. As known he ceases to be *God*. We are never outside of God so that we could set him in front of us, as an object." However, *Aphorism* 49 says of the idea of God: "This idea is not an object which can be disputed, nor can it lead to discord. ... The inane one who denies it, gives it voice without knowing it, for he cannot reasonably connect any two concepts except *in* this idea." It is, as Augustine puts it, "that whence the light of reason is lit." (See above, page 62*.) Schelling's *Aphorism* 48 says: "Reason does not *have* the idea of God, it *is* this idea, and nothing else." In this respect, one could understand the words
(85)   which the writer of *Acts* (17:28) puts in the mouth of Paul: "For in Him we live and move and have our being."

One of the thoughtless questions many still ask is: How can finite man understand infinite God? And they answer: Human reason is too weak for that! Schelling warns us: "*Weak* is not the reason which is incapable of knowing an objective God, but rather a reason which *desires* to know such a God. Because you believed that you could not act without an objective God and an absolutely objective world, it was necessary to comfort you with the talk about the weakness of your reason; then it might become possible to take away that toy of your reason; you needed the solace of a promise that you would get the toy back

(86) at some later time. One had to hope that, by that time, you
would have learned to act on your own, having finally grown up
to manhood. But when will that hope be fulfilled?" (I,290f)

This passage may be an echo from Kant's *Prolegomena* of
1783 (§46): "The human intellect is not to be blamed for not
knowing the substance of things, but for desiring to know what
is a sheer idea, as if it could be determined like an object."

As for Schelling's phrase, "that toy of your reason," our so
very advanced modern minds may be surprised to read in
Augustine's book *On True Religion*: "If we cannot yet inhere in
the eternal, let us at least not accept our phantasms and reject
from the spectacle of our mind such futile and deceptive
playthings."*

(87) It is high time that we begin to study what has long been
in the books. We may still do it before an atomic war sets
mankind back a few thousand years. For an atomic war will
deteriorate into a religious war between Marxian dogmatism and
an ostensible Christianity which dogmatically clings to an al-
legedly existing objective God.

Student Questions

(70) Q: If God is not something material which we can see
and touch, then can we ever prove that God exists? If God
exists in us then, if you acknowledge your own existence,
must you not acknowledge the existence of God?

A: We can prove and ought to prove that God is *not* an
object. The proof lies in the definition: Objects are conditioned, and a conditioned "God" would be a demon
depending on whatever "superior being" conditions him.
And if you turn that "superior being" into an object, you
have a progress *ad infinitum*. As for your second question,
which speaks of existence in a mind, you will have as many
gods as you have minds or, in polytheism, many more. But

De vera religione (L,98): Cui (aeternitati) si nondum possumus inhaerere,
obiurgemus saltem nostra phantasmata, et tam nugatorios et deceptorios *ludos* de
spectaculo mentis eiiciamus. [Schelling's word was *Spielwerk*.]

what do you mean by God existing in us? As an entity of our imagination, like a dream? Or as the unconditional challenge of which the previous chapters have spoken? If the latter, do you propose to turn the "Challenger" into a conditional objective entity?

(71) Q: Since God is a divine being, he should be able to do things that are not humanly possible. An example would be His walking on water. You say it is Bible poetry, but who can say He actually did not?

A: A poem can be addressed, even at the most respectful distance, to a woman in the flesh, like Petrarca's Laura. On the other hand, the poet's beloved may be a fiction of fancy. Surely the Beatrice who guides Dante through Purgatory and Paradise is not the very young girl with whom he fell in love as a boy. Yet even the fictitious women of poetry "actually" exist, in their poetic individuality. Nevertheless, poetry cannot and does not claim that they are identical with any living models.

The case is quite different with mythological figures. Nobody has seen Zeus seducing any one of the women with whom he fell in love, yet the Greeks credited him with having actually had his affairs. Poetry carries us away in its rapture, but it respects the difference between poetic imagination and historical reality. Mythology however demands that the believer refrain from making this distinction. I do not deny that there is "Bible poetry." As far as I can make out, the *Song of Songs* is addressed by a real lover to his real lady. I know, of course, that some churches hold that it is addressed by Christ to his beloved Church.

As for Christ walking on water, I do *not* call it Bible poetry. I do call poetry the story of the jinnee of Aladdin's lamp, for I do not believe that the writer of the story meant to report an historic event. In contrast, even if it could be proven that Matthew (14:25), Mark (6:48) and John (6:19) held the story (which Luke does not have) to be fiction, churchmen since have held it to be the report of an historical fact. I call it mythology since, as a philosopher, I have the duty to distinguish between fact and fiction and, as a physicist, I cannot dodge the question as to the physical possibility of such walking. The question is twofold. Since there is a storm, the water cannot be frozen and therefore the first question is about buoyancy. Normally the specific weight of the human body is only a little less than that of water. What then happened? Was the specific weight of the body of Jesus temporarily reduced to that of a light gas, or was the specific weight of water increased to that of mercury or of an even heavier liquid? Your willingness to waive this question amounts to a declaration that the findings of physics can be ignored, being nothing but a fiction of the human mind. You also do not take seriously a second question: Granted the buoyancy, how can one maintain one's balance while standing or walking on water? A man on water skis loses his balance as soon as he loses his speed.

I agree with your statement that "God should be able to do things that are not humanly possible." In fact, I do go farther. God can and does do what he alone can do. As far as we humans are concerned, we cannot but acknowledge the fact that we are always confronted by the challenge of the four ideas. I am quite willing to call that fact the Will of God which has unavoidable authority over us. Such authority is "not humanly possible" even in a Hitler, Stalin, or Mao. There are people who object to the phrase "Will of God" because to them it expresses the belief in a celestial dictator. Their objection is justified although they do not know why. For, as Augustine says (*De trinitate*, VIII,vii,11)*: "They try to go outside and they desert their own inwardness in whose interior is God." As for you, I ought to say with Augustine: "As I hope, God will in fact grant that I be able to answer you properly, or rather, grant that you answer yourself, being taught inwardly by the very truth which is the highest teacher of all" (*De libero arbitrio* II,ii,4).** Remember that

---

*Exterius enim conantur ire et interiora sua deserunt quibus interior est Deus.
**Donabit quidem Deus, ut spero, ut tibi valeam respondere, vel potius ut ipse tibi eadem, quae summa omnium magistra est, veritate intus docente respondeas.

for Augustine God is truth itself. And, since truth has unconditional authority, and since you feel it but cannot clearly say it, you find yourself looking outward instead of inward, and saying conditionally "God should" instead of "God does," unconditionally. What is outward is all conditional (and therefore in the domain of scientific questions) while unconditionality can be expressed mythologically only in terms of miracles (which defy scientific logic).

(72)   Q: If the Epicureans believed that nature did the punishing, is not nature then a god in a sense?

       A: Yes, if mythologized.

(73)   Q: Is the belief of an individual in the existence of God dependent on the importance of that God in the individual's life?

       A: Yes, of course.

       Q: In the same way in which the acceptance of the basic assumptions of science is dependent on the importance and role of science in the individual's life?

       A: Subjectively, yes. Objectively, the validity of scientific findings does not rest on their importance to the individual scientist. He has to produce evidence, from objective observation. Likewise, the tenable meaning of the word God is not identical with any subjective conviction of the individual believer. If it were, religious truths could be established by landslide votes. This seems to be what worries you. Just as science requires objective observation, so does philosophy require a critically tutored attention to the truth which "teaches inwardly," as Augustine says. See (71) above.

(74)   Q: As soon as you put God on a level with yourself you become idolatrous, because God is not a personage. Should I assume that God is everything that is goodness? But then what is goodness? Maybe I am looking for something that I alone must find.

A: Yes, indeed, in each case, in line with "the Will of God" which sternly demands of you personally that you determine, in conscience and in logic, just what, in the case that confronts you, *is* good—of course within the limits of your contemporary civilization (which may not be up to date) and your individual preparation (which your elders and yourself may have neglected). This marks the difference between animals who live by instinct and men who ought to live by responsibility. Or, if you will, the difference between living in paradise and living "in the world." For animals the universe has no center, but for man there is a center though he does not yet know what it it; as yet it looks like a tree bearing tempting fruit. God called it "the tree of the knowledge of good and evil," and the snake tells Eve, "God knows that the very day you eat of it, your eyes will be opened, and you will be like gods who know good from evil." (*Genesis* 2:17 and 3:5, translation by J. M. Powis Smith). Man is not a god, because his knowledge is not infallible but responsibly tentative. He himself must reach for it. And in that respect he is made in the image of God who is not a creature but, being sheer authority, is ever new spontaneity, "I shall be who shall be" (*Exodus* 3:14). Of course you are right in saying God is not a personage such as the writer of Genesis makes it appear, since mythology must dramatically objectify its insights.

(75) Q: Assuming I believe there is a God, why did he put me in this world? What are God's interests?

A: If this were the kind of study which permits examinations, I should say your first three words already indicate a failure. As long as you speak of God as an assumption you are speaking of a conditional entity in which one can but need not believe. In short, you are speaking of one of the gods, and you do not seem to realize that one can believe in such a god only as long as one endows him with the unconditional authority of God, on which man's integrity depends.

Fortunately you express your own integrity by asking, 'why am I here?' But then you relapse into conditional thinking and you ask: "What are God's interests?"

Having interests means depending on the existence of whatever happens to be interesting. And a dependent god is not God. Thomas Aquinas says "there is no passive potentiality whatever in God" (*Summa Theologica*, I, Q.16, Art.1, resp.), no possibility of being influenced, nor any want.

However, the meaning of your mythological language is plain enough, and I should answer mythologically that, your question being sincere, God wants you to ask it and also to ask the next one.

Q: Am I here to be happy, or am I here only to serve some purpose of God?

A: Why do you make it an alternative, either/or? The saints at least find their own greatest happiness in serving God.

Augustine wrote: "God loves us, but in what way? To make use of us? Or to enjoy us? But in order to enjoy us he would have to be in need of whatever is good in us, and nobody sane would say that. For, everything good in us is either God himself or is from him. Therefore he does not enjoy us but uses us." And he adds that "what is called God's use of us does not refer to any benefit of his but to ours, and it refers only to his goodness." (*De doctrina christiana*, I,xxxi,34 and 37.) Maybe this answers your last and indeed very sad question.

Q: If I am neither seeking happiness for myself here or hereafter, nor fulfilling a purpose of God, then I must assume that the same is true for other people, unless I see some reason why they are different. If they are not different, were we all put here only to eat, sleep and reproduce to perpetuate our kind? In that regard we are all merely consumers. We have no purpose except to use up the resources of this world.

A: You once told me you are a Catholic. That alone, of
course, is no guarantee that you could not find yourself in
the dull doldrums you express. Nevertheless have the saints
really forsaken you? What about the earthy joy of a St.
Francis? What about the profound thinking and lofty
enthusiasm of a St. Augustine? Surely St. Teresa of Avila
and St. Therese of Lisieux were not of the opinion that
mankind is but a rabbit warren. As for yourself, why did
you decide to become a nurse? I seem to be the wrong
doctor for you, since my preceding chapters have not been
of any help toward your liberation from the "It" thinking
which seems to be at the root of your bewilderment. The
great psychoanalyst, Carl Gustav Jung, used to send pa-
tients for whom he found himself the wrong helper to their
priest. Maybe I should do the same.

(76) Q: Man believes in a supreme being because of fear of the
unknown and on account of the weakness of his character.
Can clear thinking and reliance on mankind fulfill man's
needs?

A: Mankind is conditioned by nature and history. Religion rightly points out that man's needs go beyond the
conditional. Having in mind her unconditional concern, St.
Teresa of Avila said that, if it were for the greater glory of
God, she would gladly go to Hell, and she knew that Hell
means the irreparable separation from God. She had little
philosophical tutoring, but her thinking was quite clear
when she said that. Our century demands of us that our
thinking should be philosophically clear. We should not
indulge in wild generalizations such as your surmise that
human fears and weaknesses can furnish exhaustive explanations. And clear thinking should make us reject or at least
question all final formulations.

(77) Q: Is God, the magnificent supreme being, a dreamed up
uniqueness in man's imagination? Or: Is God a necessary,
real (real in the sense of existing in both, mankind and in
that unearthly Heaven) part of everything that has been, is,
and will be?

A: You ask as if there could be an alternative between your two questions. But the second one, in its formulation, is unintentionally something dreamed up by your imagination. You speak of God as existing in mankind, but so does every dream. And in the domain of imagination dreams are most certainly real. You speak of "that unearthly Heaven" and let it go at those words, and words are surely products of the imagination. You surmise that God could be *"part of everything,"* but the word "part" is a spatial term which keeps your problem confined to the imagination and keeps it from critical thought. And, to clinch the deal, you end with words from the Episcopal doxology, beautiful words, but not quite fit to say what you want to know. You do begin to think when you speak of God as necessarily real. But you do not insist on knowing what that could mean.

We could not be really human if we did not experience the challenge of the just, the good, the true, and the beautiful. What is nature without the truth of its laws and the beauty of its forms? What is society without justice and goodness? So at least the four ideas are necessarily real.

78)   Q: Why do we insist on changing everyone else's religious beliefs to be like our own? How do we know our red Indians were not right in worshipping the sun, for instance, and that we were not wrong in converting them to Christianity?

A: In 1779, Lessing wrote his famous play, *Nathan the Wise,* in whose central third act the Sultan Saladin asks Nathan for his opinion as to which of the three religions, Judaism, Christianity and Islam is the right one. Nathan tells him the story of the ring which had the power of making its wearer beloved by God and man, provided it was worn in good faith. The ring came down through generations, always bestowed by the father upon the son he loved most. Finally, a father had three sons whom he loved equally well. In weak moments he had promised the ring to each of the three. Before he died he had two perfect copies made which he could not himself distinguish one from the original. He gave each son a ring and died. Saladin asks how this story answers his question. And Nathan asks in return: "How can I trust my father less than you trust yours?" But Saladin wants to hear the end of the story. The three sons quarrel and finally come before the judge whose verdict is as follows. Since the power of the ring depends upon being worn in good faith, go, each one of you, wear the ring in good faith and act in that faith, hand the ring down from generation to generation, and in a thousand thousand years, let the three heirs appear in court again for, by then, the power of the genuine ring will have proven itself, unless of course all three rings were mere copies. The answer to your question is that, like most humans, the adherents of the different religions believe their fathers most, and therefore harbor the conviction that their religion is the right one. Now, if you ask my opinion, I believe the time has come to quit quarrelling about the "right" religion, and for all men to live in good faith. However, we can do so only if we give up our lazy tolerance which keeps us in ignorance of the other fellow's religion and permits us to believe that ours is better. What is required of us is the persistent dedication to study, which must replace the easy enthusiasm of missionarizing. Study will show that not all religions have the same depth in all respects but that each of those above the primitive level has its contribution to make. If these contributions are acknowledged, each owes a debt to the others, and that includes even so dubious a religion as Marxism.

(79) Q: Do you believe the credibility of the Judeo-Christian religion is seriously challenged by its similarity in myths, ideas and beliefs with the other cultures that predated it or coexisted with it in the Mediterranean Basin?

      A: I do not believe that one can speak of "*the* Judeo-Christian religion" without bogging down in utter confusion. Judaism is unitarian, Christianity trinitarian. Consequently in the geographic region to which you refer, and in the historical era which includes our time, Judaism, Islam and Unitarianism might come to a theological agreement. They surely must reject the orthodox Christian dogma that Jesus of Nazareth was the incarnation of the second person of the Trinity, that is, that God ever was a man. If you throw the two irreconcilable doctrines into a mixer, you wind up with a mess which, being nothing but a mess, could of course not be "challenged" by the different mess you seem to mix out of (which?) "myths, ideas and beliefs." Our duty as students is to leave messes alone. They are all incredible by nature. But they may appeal to people who have a taste for them.

(80)   Q: Do you believe Freud's theories concerning the psychological origin and the motives behind religion offer any serious challenge to the credibility of religion in general?

A: Yes, in objectivistic minds, that is, for people who take religion to be a piece of otherwise unobtainable information "from beyond" and who now discover that, as a psychological phenomenon, religion wells up "from within." This kind of mind still has a sound though vague feeling that there is something wrong in reducing truth to a psychological phenomenon. A courageous mind will turn this feeling into an explicit question. But timid or untutored minds are afraid of sharp questions, and also of psychological discoveries. Hence their frequent hostility to study. As for genuinely religious minds, if untutored they, too, may share the fear of study. But any sound religion will see to it that its teaching also is sound. Studies of the merely conditional cannot even touch the unconditional which is the real concern of religion. This can be made philosophically clear. But if philosophical discipline is lacking, religious soundness will manifest itself in some mythological expression. Instead of saying with the philosopher's terms that "the unconditional cannot be reduced to anything conditional," the defender of religion will say, "God is not one of the gods who are but figments of human fancy." Of course, Freud will retort that this religionist clings frantically to his illusion, which he tries to save by spelling God with a capital G. What we students ought to know and point out is that Freud lacks philosophical discipline just as much as the religionist who finds himself restricted to the use of mythological terms.

(81) Q: I find myself visualizing God in my mind. I am not saying that God has to be a person with a certain image. He may be immaterial, but I have a need to relate to an image. Is this plausible?

A: Yes, it is even inevitable as long as you have not clearly understood that, first, all understanding and all communication must be articulate and thus requires imagery, and second, that images can only furnish masks for the unconditional, which demands of us that we discard any given image for a better one. Any image which poses as the definitive likeness of God is an idol. Hence the Second Commandment, once it is lifted out of the context of polytheism and interpreted to mean that man ought not to make any image of God. To be sure, as long as you do not also clearly understand that there is no objective God, the very word God can take the nature of a forbidden image. Hence the Jewish habit of replacing the holy name by the circumlocution "he whose name be praised." Hence also the stress which the church puts on "the hidden God," *deus absconditus.* Yet somehow you need to speak.

(82) Q: Does Paul Tillich's expression "ultimate concern" or "unconditional concern" change the traditional meaning of the word "God" so that an atheist cannot really exist?

A: It seems obvious that your phrase "the traditional meaning" refers to the objectivistic assumption that God is something or some personage "out there." In that case, it is not only Tillich in our century but, for instance, Augustine, over a millennium and a half ago, who challenges that meaning. See the quotations in (71) above. The challenge had been made even another millennium earlier, by the Psalmist (14:1 and 53:1) who calls him who says, "there is no God," a fool which, according to St. Jerome's Vulgate, is *insipiens*, that is, one who does not *know* what he is talking about. We, for the sake of our being human, are challenged to *know* the truth. But what if you have doubts? Augustine says: "Everyone who understands that he is doubting knows something that is true, and he is certain of this fact. Everyone, therefore, who doubts there is any truth has in himself something true of which he does not doubt. Nor is anything true except the truth. Therefore he who can doubt at all ought not to doubt of the truth." For it is not he who has produced this certainty that he is doubting; "ratiocination cannot produce this kind of fact, it finds it."* And as one who doubts, he is seeking the truth which he loves. "Anyone who can love at all, loves God, whether he knows it or not."** The sincere atheist is just such a lover who does not know it. But anyone who is not sincere and therefore does not care, is not of a pure mind. And "God did not want anyone but the pure to *know* what is true."**

(83)   Q: You have stated that God and truth are one and inseparable. You have also stated that even atheists and agnostics worship the truth. Does this mean that atheists and agnostics could really be worshipping God while they claim there is none?

       A: Yes, indeed. See (82)**—I merely quoted Augustine who, to be sure, presents no reversible identity, so that one could say, going one way, God is the truth, and going the other way, the truth is God. Instead of formulating such a flat identity, he says: "If there is anything more excellent (than the truth) that rather is God, but if there isn't then the truth itself is already God. But either way, you cannot

---

*Omnis qui se dubitantem intelligit, verum intelligit, et de hac re quam intelligit certus est: de vero igitur certus est. Omnis igitur qui utrum sit veritas dubitat, in seipso habet verum unde non dubitet; nec ullum verum nisi veritate verum est. Non itaque oportet eum de veritate dubitare, qui potuit undecumque dubitare, ... Non enim ratiocinatio talia facit, sed invenit. (*De vera religione,* xxxix,73)

**Deus, quem amat omne quod potest amare, sive sciens, sive nesciens. ... Deus, qui nisi mundos verum scire noluisti. (*Soliloquia,* I,i,2)

deny that God is."* I have never considered agnostics to be as sincere as atheists. Atheists want nothing except the truth. Agnostics merely abstain from seeking. All they seek is excuses, for instance they say that human reason is too weak to find God. (See the Schelling quotation I,290, our page 93f). They do not really love the truth. Atheists do. But that does not mean they "worship God." How can anyone worship that of which he says it *is* not in any way? Some agnostics, however, do worship what they call the unknowable. That word may designate God from a safe distance; so the worship surely is not very fervent.

(84) Q: Religion is to answer man's questions about the un-answerable. What is the purpose of philosophy?

A: It is to do away with such obvious contradictions as your "answering the unanswerable." Such expressions may stun unprepared minds and stop them from deeper inquiry, but they shed no light on the problem. Philosophy asks: "Unanswerable by whom?" And it replies: "Unanswerable by a ratiocinating reason which would turn the uncondi-tionality of God into an object, that is, something condi-tioned; a reason which seeks impersonal proofs instead of personal insight." When religion brings forward its answers they appeal to insight, they are unintelligible to ratio-cination.

(85) Q: In your own opinion, how can a person really "live in him" when he is being tortured by him? In modern language, wouldn't we call this masochistic?

A: Yes, if psychological terminology could reach the depth of the matter. The question is what do you mean by being tortured by God? Physical suffering, for instance a painful disease? Depending on the patient's stamina, even that can be borne. A believer may say, "God wants it so, and who am I to argue?" Or do you mean that mental torture which Karl Rahner has so beautifully expressed in

---

*Si enim aliquid est excellentius, ille potius Deus est: si autem non est, iam ipsa veritas Deus est. Sive ergo illud sit, sive non non sit, Deum tamen esse, negare non poteris. (*De libero arbitrio,* xii ff.)

his little prayer book, *Words Spoken Into Silence,* the "silence éternel de la divinité" as Alfred de Vigny called it. "Show me thy face!" pleads Moses; and the answer is, "you can see me only from the back" [when I have already passed by! See our page 35.] In either case, the faithful persists in this trust and so "lives in God."

(86) Q: At this point I still do not know how to approach God. Will this concept become clearer to me as I go on?

A: I hope so. You may be perplexed by the eternal silence of divinity. See (85). But ours is not a revival meeting. As "men of God," preachers are supposed to be healers, even saviors. But professors are merely students who have been granted time to read a little more. Don't lose courage, and keep reading. For instance, read what Schelling says when he points out that man does not *come* to God, but the very first move of his consciousness is *away* from God. (XII,120.) For, in order to be aware of anything, we must put it before us so that it can confront our mind. Therefore we have the natural tendency to seek God outside. But Augustine warns us "do not go outside; go back into yourself; in the inner man dwells truth." (See above p. 62*.)

(87) Q: If religion gives man security and some peace of mind, what reason can be given for religious wars.

A: Dogmatism, in the technical philosophic sense, that is, taking myths literally. For instance taking literally the mythological hope of Marx that world communism will surely come, and will be followed by the classless society. And on this side of the "iron curtain" (which nowadays we should call the bone curtain, meaning the boneheads) taking literally the belief that the world can be saved only by everybody becoming "a Christian." If we do that, we have an impass, and the boneheads will tell us it can be broken by bombing. These poor untutored minds cannot see that the real solution is knowing each other, and talking with each other instead of shooting at each other, like the poor people in Ulster.

Chapter VII

POSITIVE AND NEGATIVE THEOLOGY

The Cardinal Nicolaus Cusanus (1401-1464) wrote *De docta ignorantia (On Learned Ignorance)* in 1440. I translate from

Chapter 24: *"Since God is the One in its totality, he can have no power name, for it would be necessary to give him every name or to name everything by God's name, since in this simplicity he comprehends the totality of things. ... But since the name of God is God, it can be known only by a reason (intellectus) which is itself the maximum and the maximal name. Therefore, in the learned ignorance, we find that, though Unity seems to be the word closest to the name of the maximum, it is still infinitely far from the true name of the maximum. Accordingly, all names which we give God affirmatively, pertain to him only in an infinitely minute degree, for we attribute them to God in line with what we find in creatures. ... What we said about affirmative names is so true that even the name of Trinity is imposed upon God only with regard to his relation to creatures, that is, the name of the Father, the Son, and the Holy Spirit."*

From Chapter 26: *"Since every worship of God, who must be adored in spirit and in truth [John 4:24], has its necessary foundation in positive affirmations regarding God, therefore every religion ascends by means of positive theology, [for instance] adoring God as one and tri-une, as wisest and holiest, as unapprochable light [I Tim. 6:16], as life, truth, and similar designations. In so doing, religion directs worship by faith which it attains more truly by learned ignorance [rather than argumentation]. When religion worships God as inaccessible light, what is meant, of course, is not a physical light whose contrast is darkness, but that most simple and non-finite 'light' in which the very darkness is non-finite light. This light shines always in the darkness of our ignorance, although this ignorance cannot comprehend it [John 1:5]. And so, negative theol-*

ogy is indispensable as a completion of positive, because without it God would not be worshipped as non-finite but rather as a creature, and this latter kind of worship is idolatry since it renders to the image what pertains only to the truth. ... According to this negative theology, God is neither Father, nor Son, nor Holy Spirit, but only non-finite."

Let us ignore for the moment the trinitarian question and consider instead what the Cusan has to say about "light." The figurative use of the word is old. In the parable of the Den (*Republic 515e*), Plato speaks of "the light itself" (autò tò phōs), meaning the light of truth in which we can see what, in our previous ignorance, we could not. In the *Book of Job* (33:28) we read that the merciful God will deliver the sinner's soul from annihilation so that "his life shall see the light." (Jerome translates: *vivens lucem videret,* so that, as a living one, he may see the light.) The Christ of *John* (8:12) says: "I am the light of the world. He who followeth me shall not walk in the darkness but shall have the light of life."

It is obvious to every but the most naive reader that the "light" of truth or of life is not physical and that it would be absurd to inquire about its wave length or its candle power. In this case only a single-track materialistic mind could miss the insight of "negative theology" that "light" is not to be taken literally but figuratively.

However when Cusanus says that, in the light of truth, "the very darkness is non-finite light," the meaning is not immediately obvious. It is obvious enough that our ignorance cannot annihilate the truth, which "shines always." Often we are not aware of the fact that we are "in the dark"; we are under the delusion that we know when, in fact, we do not know. But this mistaken belief of ours is still a belief, that is, it claims to be true and thus refers to truth. In the form of this implicit reference the light of truth "shines" in our darkness of mind, though as yet invisible to us, not yet explicit. As soon as we voice that fact, in definite words, the very finiteness of such articulation manifests the non-finiteness of the light of truth. Truth is manifest in our finite articulations of it, but they cannot turn it into a finite entity. It is not identical with our

(88)

verbal expressions. As soon as we succeed in making a meaning-ful statement, the very "idea" of truth demands that we check and restate our finding, in order not to kill and bury it in our verbiage.

(89)   There is nothing inherently wrong with the poetic terms of positive theology. Even negative theology has to use terms, and its expressions like those of positive theology are in danger of being taken literally and thus misinterpreted. Formulations are finite, the truth is non-finite. Cusanus still uses the word infinite, but I translate his *lux infinita* as non-finite light. Thus his own sentences furnish an example of what he means by negative theology verifying positive theology. The word infinite might mislead us into the endlessness of space or time, which Hegel called the "bad infinity" (V,97) and which would make the "positive" statement of Cusanus meaningless.

What could the phrase "infinite light" mean? Surely not the blinding flash of an atomic explosion. The sun is brighter, and even a new star, a *nova,* is not "infinitely" bright.

All measurements are finite. When we speak of the infinity of space we mean that a further step of measurement is always possible beyond every definite and therefore finite point our measuring has reached. Likewise the positing of such points can go on endlessly in counting whole numbers: $1, 2, 3, \ldots, (n-1)$, $n, (n+1)$. There is no final number but always one more than the one just reached: $(n+1)$. It is impossible to count out "all" the numbers, therefore it would be a hopeless undertaking. The assignment would amount to being condemned to an unending job like the one imposed by Zeus on Sisyphus whose stone always rolled down the hill after he had pushed it up. It would be hell. Yet, is not this "bad infinity" one of the traits of our world?

Religious hope, therefore, speaks of an *end* of the world, and of the peace of heaven. These are soothing words. They offer positive hope which, however, is snatched away as soon as ratiocination brings back the "bad infinity," with its endlessness. Then the word "eternity" comes to signify the very endless time which is "of the world," and heaven threatens to become a boredom, even a hell.

Religious fervor wants salvation now, and one mystic said

that to be with God for the length of time between two blinks of our eyelids would be far more blessed than all eternity in heaven. Can "all time" afford any blessing?

No "worldly" terms can satisfy the religious aspiration. Therefore mythological language must point beyond the "bad infinity," and what the great myths of the religions meant to bring within reach of the human mind was really the non-finite. The negation of the finite is always implied. There is no real religion without this negation.

John the Baptist preaches that "the Kingdom of Heaven is coming" (*Matthew* 3:2; Goodspeed translation; Luther translates "ist nahe herbeigekommen," has come close) but when he sends word from prison, the answer sent back by Jesus implies that the Kingdom is here already (*Matthew* 11:3 and *Luke* 7:22). It is the positive theologians, the literalist scribes who "shut the kingdom of heaven against men" (*Matthew* 23:13). This is not their intention but it is the effect of positive theology not corrected by negative.

(90)   Positive theology takes myth as a vision of what is real. Negative theology reminds us of the symbolism of myth which must not be taken literally.

One might say that a genuine student must learn the technique of reading myths properly. But there can be no passkey technique. It is always case work. The right interpretation depends on one's knowledge of history, that is, of the cultural climate in which the myth arose, and of the ever changing meaning of words. One must study case by case. Nor must one believe that there could be any finished formulae (91)   which philosophy could or should offer. After all, even in the field of philosophy itself, the terminology has a mythological touch; the use of the terms and their meaning changes, and the interpretation is an ever new task. This latter statement, to be sure, is final, but it is abstract and defines nothing in particular. Meaningful definitions depend on the topic at hand.

(92)   State the need of ever new interpretation by translating it back into the language of positive theology, and you have the doctrine of the hidden God. The positive theologian rightly tells you that, no matter how much light the dogmas may bring to your mind, there always remains the mystery of the *Deus*

absconditus. Of course you must read this last phrase, "the hidden God," not in the sense of "hiding," nor of "secretly deserting one's post" (which is one of the dictionary meanings of "abscond"). The positive theologian tells you that it is precisely the "hidden God" who is manifest in revelations and that, therefore, the manifestations can be trusted and are not dissembling pronouncements. Because of his trust, the positive theologian then takes that dubious step of accepting the revelations literally. And that is the point where negative theology becomes indispensable. It is already at work in coining the very phrase, "the hidden God."

(93)   The positive statements of theology (in our civilization, theology usually means positive theology) always bring with them the possibility of our misreading them (just as our civilization often misreads philosophical terms), as if the "sacred" words could contain the truth once and for all. Such a contained truth would be like the illusory life bestowed on stuffed animals by a good taxidermist. Museum animals do not really live. Animals can be killed, the truth cannot. Animals are finite, the truth is non-finite. After Kant and Hegel one must be careful and not say infinite for non-finite.

When Cusanus speaks of "that most simple and *infinite* light in which the very darkness is infinite light" (lucem simplicissimam et infinitam, in qua tenebrae sunt lux infinita) he may be thinking of the "inaccessible light" in which dwells the Lord (*I Timothy* 6:16), who veils himself "in light as in a garment" (*Psalm* 104:2). At all events, Cusanus started by saying he is not speaking of "a physical light whose contrast is darkness." He knows he is speaking figuratively. The word "light" is symbolic, as in *Psalm* 27:1, "the Lord is my light," or in *John* 1:9, "the true light that enlightens every man," and the two verses where the Christ of John says "I have come as a light into the world" (12:46) and "I am the light of the world" (8:12).

If you visualize this symbolic light you have a mythological image. In 1854, the Pre-Raphaelite Holman Hunt (1827-1909) produced a creditable painting with the title "The Light of the World." An elaborate lantern hangs at knee height from Christ's left hand and sheds a soft light over the lower part of his long robe. A perfectly circular halo stands like a moon directly behind his crowned head, but his face is lit by a dim radiance which seems to emanate from the face itself rather than from the lamp below. His right hand is knocking at a door which, of course, is an allegory of the attitude of man's soul which as yet locks out the Savior. If the beholder is a believer he will confess that this being locked is still the sorry condition of his own soul and, for him, the picture will be a sermon in paint. It must be understood symbolically. The nonbeliever may admire the composition and appreciate the mood; he may even experience an empathy with the believing Christian. But if either of them should take literally what the picture shows objectively, unanswerable questions would pop up. Do not saints wear their halos horizontally above their heads, like hovering luminous rings? Is Hunt's vertical disk an intrusion into the picture, an expression of his intellectual protest against the Renaissance fashion of wearing halos, and a decided return to medieval vertical ones? Or what does the disk do, objectively? It is right behind the head and cannot be the moon. And whence the lamp? From Diogenes who used one in bright daylight, looking for a true man on the market place of Athens? Where does Scripture tell of Jesus carrying a lamp? Furthermore, can John's trinitarian "Light of the World" be reconciled with the unitarian verse quoted above from *Psalm* 104:2?

With the latter question you find yourself in the domain of textual criticism which duly deals with historical problems, but which the cautious believer would prefer not to enter, lest his set of beliefs be disturbed. Like pictures and myths, the elaborations of the latter, resulting in beliefs and dogmas must be taken symbolically, as indeed the faithful will take them, calling them sacred. This does not require an explicit awareness of negative theology. It is enough that the doctrines be sacred, that is, that the believer refrain from asking secular questions about them. In the book *On the Trinity* (V,i,2) Augustine warns us that the godhead "must not be measured after the custom of things visible, and mutable, and mortal, and not self-sufficient," and that man, "though he cannot yet find out in all ways what God is, nevertheless he piously takes heed, as much as he is able, to think nothing of Him that He is not." (Martindales' translation.) This taking heed is negative theology. So is Augustine's warning against "futile and deceptive plays" of our intellect (*De vera religione*, 50:98).

(94)   Such deceptions lead to doubt. Doubt, however, is no futile game, as Augustine stresses in many passages, for instance in the two quoted on page 12 above. Depending on the circumstances, doubt is the very way to truth. Without a pertinent question there can be no meaningful answer. (Reading even as little as the pages of this text, you may have found yourself at a loss, here and there, simply because you could not raise the pertinent question, in your mind.) Doubt is one form of negative theology, a form of seeking truth. "And ye shall seek me and find me when ye shall search for me with all your heart." (*Jer.* 29:13).

Your not facing a question which has struck your mind does not make it vanish. Questions demand answers. And if an image put before you by positive theology has evoked a question in your mind, the mere gazing at the image is not likely to bring forth a tenable answer. It is all very well to be told: Keep praying! But prayers are no magical incantations. Prayer is effective only if spoken from unshaken faith. But if beliefs have come to be untenable and have affected the firmness of the faith, prayer is no longer an affirmation of faith, but an outcry for help. A man "fallen from faith" cannot get it back by empty will. Petulant persistence is childish. A mature mind will look for help where it is available. The Church speaks of the help from the saints. And some believers harbor a picture of a celestial police or a lost and found department. "Dear Saint Anthony, help me find the ring I misplaced!" Well, if you really believe in the busy saint, your trust may quiet your frantic search and, with a more relaxed mind you may suddenly remember where you put the ring.

How do you find a lost faith again? Do let "the saints" help you. Their number not only includes the writers of the (95)   Bible and of other religious literature but, when it comes to negative theology, you can consider the pertinent philosophers as helpful saints. Only, in that case, the anguished outcry for help is not enough. You must contribute what you do have by (96)   way of a contribution, namely as clear cut a question as you can formulate. And then, of course, you require the necessary bibliographic knowledge, whom to consult, and in which passages of which books; and that will make possible the other half of your contribution: persistent study!

Dear Reader:

I can almost hear you exclaim: "Study what?" If all you want is a random mention of good readings, let me refer you first to the famous Jewish scholar, Martin Buber. Then there is a very good book by Hans Urs von Balthaser, *The God Question and Modern Man* (Seabury Press, New York 1958). Balthaser is a Catholic but this book is addressed to any serious thinker. If you want to tackle something very thorough though not easy, take the first volume of Paul Tillich's *Systematic Theology* (University of Chicago Press 1951).

But you are on your own and you may already have consulted some of the authors quoted in this book.

At all events, do not forget Augustine's advice: "It is our task to consider carefully which authors or which books to believe in order properly to devote ourselves to God in whom alone is our soundness."*

This advice may remind you of Socrates' warning to young Hippocrates quoted on our first page, and you rightly ask me in what way one can be careful in considering books. With that question you appoint me as your tutor. But since we are not in correspondence my tutorial advice must be brief and sound rather personal.

We have already found that reason does not deal with the abstract, as does the intellect in certain fields of study, but with concrete, specific, personal questions. Hegel has said in the introduction to his *History of Philosophy* (XIII,37): "Philosophy is most inimical to the abstract; it leads back to the concrete." This sentence of his terminates a long explanatory paragraph which you may want to read for the sake of concreteness.

An absentee tutor must let things go at such literary hints.

De vera religione xxv,46: Sed nostrum est considerare quibus vel hominibus vel libris credendum sit ad colendum recte Deum quae una salus est.

And since he is only human, he must rest his advice on his own experience. What I am going to say here may sound presumptive. However it is not arrogance which makes me offer you a list of authors worth consulting. I myself have found them helpful and, in fact, I feel that without their help one is barred from the most decisive insights of occidental philosophy. Other tutors will undoubtedly add to my list and they might even dispute one name or another on it. We are not in an ecclesiastic court trying to sever the saved from the mass of perdition. Our task is study and teaching, though the latter be restricted to advice about reading.

Here then, in short, is my personal way of deciding whether a book on philosophy of religion is worth reading or not. I turn to the index and see whether the author has quoted or referred to any one of the following thinkers, and how often. If he has not consulted any from this list of mine, I lay his book aside as not being up to date. By doing so, I may be ignoring a book of real importance. In abstract theory this is a logical possibility. In concrete history of thought, however, my loss is most unlikely, since important thinkers have always kept in mind their great predecessors. I am offering my own rule of thumb as nothing but a device which has helped me. And here is my list:

Xenophanes   Master Eckehart
Heraclitus   Nicolaus Cusanus
Parmenides   Spinoza
Plato (whose teacher Socrates   Vico
    wrote nothing)   Kant
Aristotle   Herder
Plotinus   Fichte
Augustine   Hegel
Thomas Aquinas   Schelling

Recent authors: Friedrich Nietzsche   1844-1900
                     Lucien Lévy-Bruhl   1857-1939
                     Henri Bergson   1859-1941
                     Ernst Cassirer   1874-1945
                     Fritz Medicus   1876-1956
                     Martin Buber   1878-1965

Paul Tillich   1886-1965
Erich Przywara   1889-1972

Contemporaries: Gabriel Marcel
                  Karl Rahner
                  Hans Urs von Balthaser

Student Questions

(88) Q: Questioning religious views is sometimes considered
        undesirable, but questioning an idea in itself is an indica-
        tion of an awareness of the idea. Is this a case where a
        belief, no matter whether true or false, "claims to be true
        and thus refers to truth"?

      A: Quite so. Why would anyone question a religious view
        if he were not seeking what is true? Of course, he might be
        an idler seeking nothing but argumentation, for a pastime
        or for the cussedness of it. But then his questioning would
        not be serious. It would not be a real question but only a
        pretense.

(89) Q: Some people are not able to conceive of God except
        in anthropomorphic images. Would it not be a greater
        injustice to them to remove this crutch of theirs rather
        than letting them perpetuate their "false" idea of God?

      A: You are right, and the church has pointed out the
        injustice of it, saying with the words of *Matthew* 18:6 that,
        for him who disturbs the "little ones" it would be better
        "to have a great millstone hung around his neck" and "be
        drowned in the depths of the sea." And these "little ones"
        need not be children. They may be 30 or 40 or 70. But
        does it follow that the consideration due them requires the
        neglect of those who are growing up? Would not that be an
        equally intolerable injustice? Paul says: "When I was a
        child, I felt as a child, I thought as a child. Now that I
        have become a man, I have put away the things of a child."
        (*I Corinthians* 13:11)

(90) **Q:**   The Catholic Church speaks of the unlimited saving power of the grace of Christ in case of "sincere ignorance" of its doctrines. The latter, if I understand correctly, are positive theology. Turning the matter the other way around, what could be said of those who are in sincere ignorance of the teaching of negative theology that "myth must not be taken literally"?

    A: My answer would be much the same as (89) above.

(91) **Q:**   Why is it so necessary to ask a question in philosophical language? If a person has a question, isn't it better to ask it in his own words as it is in his mind, rather than to distort the question by putting it in philosophical jargon?

    A: The jargon of any discipline is only a time saver and cannot by itself answer any question. The classical chemist used to define the atom as the last indivisible particle in the form of which matter occurs. And if atoms combine in relatively stable clusters, he calls that a compound, in distinction from a mere mixture. Among chemists it would be a waste of time to repeat the definitions instead of using the three jargon words. First comes the investigation and as a result the definition. Then only come the jargon terms, for instance "positive" and "negative" theology. If you use them in talking to the uninformed you merely make yourself unintelligible. So you are quite right in saying that a real question must be asked in one's own words. And I should call that the philosophical way of asking, in distinction from a merely argumentative way which is not sincere. See (88) above. To be sure, the strict discipline of philosophy, like any other discipline finds it convenient to use sharply defined jargon words or phrases instead of wasting time repeating the lengthier phrasing of sincere questioners over and over again. But without the sincerity of those questioners there would be no real problem for discussion. The questioners themselves may come to adopt the jargon as a convenience. But they may also fall for the temptation of replacing the question with verbiage.

(92)   Q: I fail to see what the translation of a religious document has to do with positive or negative theology. Is there a connection?

A: Let us take as simple an example as possible. The writer of the fourth Gospel wrote *pneûma ho theós* (*John* 4:24) and St. Jerome correctly translated *spiritus est Deus.* So did Luther: *Gott ist Geist.* The theological question asks: *What* is God? (e.g., a gas? a personage?) And the answer of John is: *pneûma, spiritus, Geist.* That, of course, leads immediately to the questions: Just exactly what does each one of these three mean? The Greek *pneûma* could mean air (as in pneumatic tires) or wind or breath, and so could the Latin *spiritus.* The latter could also mean a mood, as "being in high spirits" or low. But is God any of these things? And that is what any serious theologian wants to know. Now, the translators of King James I wrote: "God is a spirit." And this mistranslation is still repeated in the Revised edition. But the phrase "*a* spirit" induces almost every guileless reader to conceive of one spirit among many others. In English "a spirit" can also mean a ghost, even a sprite, an elf, a fairy, a goblin, and therefore a potentially malevolent agent. Does John mean that, among spirits, God is one or the one who is always benevolent? Many a Bible reader assumes that. The assumption would be a crude form of positive theology. (This does not imply that all doctrines of positive theology are crude.) Sensing that there may be something wrong in so crude a belief, negative theology puts down a question mark, as a first reminder. And then it investigates the text and its logical or illogical implications. In our times such investigations have resulted in getting rid of the misleading "a," maybe taking the cue from Jerome and Luther. Goodspeed wrote "God is spirit" (University of Chicago Press, 1939), and you find the same correct translation in the modern Catholic New Testament (St. Anthony Guild Press, Paterson, N.J. 1941). This alone can make good theological sense, which is what negative theology seeks in order to get rid of misleading rash formulations of positive theologians. (In German *ein Geist* means *a* spirit, a ghost, like *Poltergeist* or hobgoblin.)

(93) Q: Many of my friends ask: Isn't the Bible full of errors? If they are right, how can I reconcile my faith with the fact that the Bible is so contradictory?

A: Look at the table of contents of your Bible and you find 22 books from Genesis through the Song of Songs, with at least fifteen authors, and then seventeen prophets. Even if you reckon only one author for the Pentateuch, you come out with at least thirty-two for the Old Testament, but more probably over three dozen. In the New Testament you have the four Gospels. You may wish to follow church tradition and attribute Acts to Luke. Then you have the letters of Paul, James, Peter, John, Jude, and finally Revelation. Even if in line with tradition you count only one author for the Gospel of John, his letters and Revelation and attribute Hebrews to Paul, you still have at least eight authors, but more likely over a dozen. In short you are confronted with at least forty authors, and possibly well over fifty, not counting the Old and New Testament Apocrypha. As for the time of composition, some scholars date the Song of Deborah (*Judges* 5) as early as 1250 B.C. and Psalms 44, 74, 79, 83 and 110 as late as the Maccabees, 167-163 B.C.; the whole Old Testament therefore covers a millenium, and the New at least a century. Now how can you expect forty or fifty writers, the first and last a thousand years apart, to agree in every respect? How can you call their disagreements errors? You would have to declare, for instance, that the latest was right, as one might perhaps declare with regard to writers on natural science. Or you might feel like declaring the first was right, being closest to God, like Moses. But such declarations are interpretations. You do not read them *in* the Bible. To be sure, being honest men, these writers would not put down what they personally doubted. Once you admit that the Bible is a collection of books, not one book, your question vanishes. That is, you must ask it differently, starting from any one pair of "contradictory" statements. For instance, the words "I and the Father are one" (*John* 10:30) flatly contradicts "I speak not on my own authority" (*John* 14:10). You are right in pointing out the words which immediately follow: "But the Father dwelling in me, it is he who does the works." Still, these very words leave the question as to the distinction (though not separation) between Father and Son, a question that led to the Arian heresy which declared the Son to be only similar in substance to the Father, and the Athanasian orthodoxy which, at the Councils of Nicea, 325 A.D., and Constantinople, 381 A.D. declared for one and the same substance of the godhead. So you see that such "contradictions" lead (and have always led) to ecclesiastic "definitions" held to be orthodox in contrast to the beliefs of those who "stood apart" (which is what the word heretic means). As for your "faith" do not rashly identify it with your beliefs which raise questions. The churches advise their faithful to abide by the respective ecclesiastic decisions. This is a great comfort for those who can so abide. But others, who cannot squelch their sincere questions must start the laborious journey of study in the firm faith that the truth cannot be squelched though, as individuals, we may not reach the end of the tunnel. This is why the Church speaks of the beatific vision beyond our death.

(94) Q: If doubt is really a desire to find the truth then why do people (many people) allow doubt or doubts to overpower them and block the pathway to the very truth they seek?

A: Because they see no helping hands. That is the tragedy of our age. The helping hands are there, reaching out of the books in the libraries. But the books might as well be locked up in some underground safe, since neither churches nor schools tell people the books are there. This gives doubts an overpowering force whereas, in truth, doubts are not roadblocks but keys to unlock the treasures accumulated in religious and intellectual history. The church does not teach a doctrine without meaning when it says that the saints brought forth supererogatory works, that is, works going farther than what could be demanded from an individual. For, as the Church also teaches, it was Grace (bringing help to everybody) which produced the works, and not the mere effort of the saint (who surely did make his greatest effort). Great thinkers need not be canonized to help the one plagued by doubt. Unfortunately the churches seldom encourage doubters to consult even the writings of canonized saints, and they often advise the doubter to keep away from the help offered by secular thinkers.

(95) Q: Is the Bible a good source as the basis of arguments for religion (as faith)?

A: Yes, provided you consult it as a conscientious student and do not exploit it as a fanatic partisan. The latter rushes into some halfbaked positive theology. The student knows the indispensable value of negative theology. See (92) and (93) above and, of course, our whole treatise. But let me add a word of caution. I do not like your phrase "the basis of arguments." True, our statements, for instance the statements of my treatise, have the form of arguments. But that does not mean that we are here indulging in a debate in which each protagonist argues for the sake of winning. That kind of argument is selfish and hollow. A serious argument seeks truth, not victory.

(96) Q: In all the churches I have been in, I have noticed that the extent of Bible study or church service has been either the history of the Old Testament or the magic of the New Testament. I have only once heard a theologian teaching his people to search for the deeper meanings of their religion. If only a small group are developing any depth in their belief and if the rest of the people are only hitting the top, never getting past elementary stories, how can the latter group really develop a deep faith in their beliefs?

A: You have already given the sad answer: They cannot for they stand still. However, if you want my fallible opinion, I am very optimistic with regard to the present cultural thaw among American youth. We students may yet reach the point where the people will be glad to have the help of our findings which, by Grace, we may be able to locate in the written records, or formulate in plain intelligible language. Plain speech is required if we want to develop depth.

INDEX

NAMES

Aeschylus, 35
Aristotle, 40, 77f, 92
Augustine, 4f, 9, 12, 38, 49, 53, 55f, 61,
  66, 71, 81f, 85, 87, 93-99, 104ff, 113ff
Balthasar, 72, 115
W. J. Bryan, 33
Buber, 48, 115
Cassirer, 33
Counts, 80
Cusanus, 108ff, 112
Darrow, 33
Descartes, 16, 67
Fichte, ix, 1, 8, 14ff, 21, 33, 36, 39f, 87
Francis of Assisi, 83
Freud, 36, 68, 103f
Friedenberg, 2
Galilei, 88
Goethe, 35, 76
Hegel, ix, 46f, 59, 88, 110, 112, 115
Heraclitus, 14f, 41, 58
Herder, 33
Hitler, 45, 56, 96
Hobbes, 69
Jefferson, 58
Joan of Arc, 48
John Ev., 61, 71, 109, 112, 119
Kant, ix, 18, 29, 31ff, 36, 40, 50, 58f, 60,
  94, 112

Lucretius, 10
Mao, 96
Marx, 9, 50f
Medicus, 28, 55, 68
Mencken, 43
Nietzsche, 9, 11, 19, 38
Paul, 13, 41, 82, 117
Plato, 1, 31, 44, 57-61, 69, 71, 80, 109
Plotinus, 82
K. Rahner, 106
Sartre, 16
Schelling, ix, 2, 9, 22, 33, 93f
Schiller, 72
Schopenhauer, 79
Shaftesbury, 72
G. B. Shaw, 48
Socrates, 31, 115
Bernadette Soubirou, 48
Stalin, 96
Teresa of Avila, 100
Thérèse of Lisieux, 100
Thomas Aquinas, 92, 99
Tillich, 68, 75, 88, 104, 115
Vico, 32f
Xenophanes, 31
Zarathustra, 9, 11, 19, 38

TOPICS

aesthetic poverty, 72
adolescence, 2, 29, 58
art, 79
atheism, 38, 104f

authoritarianism, 57, 71, 80f, 91
authority, 57
authority of ideas, 59
authority of questions, 3, 114, 117

125

bad books, 5f
the beautiful, 72
the Bible, 120f, 123
Buddhism, 51
catechism, 63
challenge of ideas, 69, 73-77
childhood, 29f
Christ, 34, 37, 39, 71, 95, 109, 112f
church as critic of state, 7
church as routine, 63f
poor churchmen, 72
communism, 107
conformity, 78f, 86f
conscience, 78
conversion, 9f
corrupt state, 70
Creator, 90
definitions, 69, 73, 78, 121
Devil, 13, 24, 35, 48, 76
doctrine, life of a, 56
dogma, 51ff
dogmatism, 107
doubt, 12, 18, 27, 46f, 63f, 114, 121f
education, general public, 58
empathy, 17f
existence, 89
feelings, 3
finding oneself, 2
force, 71
formula, 77f
God, an arbitrary God, 51
    is beauty, 4
    consciousness moves away from God, 9
    dead, 2, 8
    eye of God, 78
    is the life of the soul, 5
    is not an object, 93
    a part time God, 66
    a personal God, 4
    the presence of God, 35
    is truth, 4, 5
    What comes from God?, 48
    the Will of God, 26, 74, 77, 96, 98
    the word "God," 49, 87, 90, 100, 104
    the wrath of God, 92
the gods, 76, 80, 91f
good, 2
the Good, 60

Grace, 51, 122f
groups, 78f
Hasidim, 9
the herd, 11
honesty of children, 62
I as a self, 13-17, 20-23, 36, 40
ideas, 43f, 46, 48, 56f, 60
the idea of ideas, 60f
idea of justice, goodness, truth, beauty, 68-73, 84
idolatry, 97, 104, 109
illumination, 85f
incarnation, 17
indoctrination, 71, 78
infinite, 110, 112
interests, 98f
irreligiosity, 44, 49, 54, 62
jargon, 118
Jesus Freaks, 3
justice, 69f
language, 2
lava in the moon, 8
law, 69
literal interpretation, 108, 110f
maturity, 2, 29
Marxism, 5, 39, 46, 50f
me, 15, 17, 23-25
memorizing, 63f, 80
miracles, 97
mystery, 49
mystery of life, 17, 25
mythological formulae, 8
mythological imagery, 8, 111
mythology, study of, 32f
Nazi, 9, 91
non-finite, 110ff
obedience, 19, 71
objectivism, 8, 36
objects are conditional, 93f
omniscience, 69
organization man, 57
organized religion, 10, 43, 49, 53
ought, 60
papal infallibility, 39
parrot, 65
personal identity, 13
philosophy, 4, 21, 53, 61, 106, 111
power, 69
power of the gods, 76
prayer, 50, 114